Serverless Swift

Apache OpenWhisk for iOS developers

Marek Sadowski
Lennart Frantzell

Apress®

Serverless Swift: Apache OpenWhisk for iOS developers

Marek Sadowski
Walnut Creek, CA, USA

Lennart Frantzell
Sunnyvale, CA, USA

ISBN-13 (pbk): 978-1-4842-5835-4
https://doi.org/10.1007/978-1-4842-5836-1

ISBN-13 (electronic): 978-1-4842-5836-1

Copyright © 2020 by Marek Sadowski and Lennart Frantzell

This work is subject to copyright. All rights are reserved by the Publisher, whether the whole or part of the material is concerned, specifically the rights of translation, reprinting, reuse of illustrations, recitation, broadcasting, reproduction on microfilms or in any other physical way, and transmission or information storage and retrieval, electronic adaptation, computer software, or by similar or dissimilar methodology now known or hereafter developed.

Trademarked names, logos, and images may appear in this book. Rather than use a trademark symbol with every occurrence of a trademarked name, logo, or image we use the names, logos, and images only in an editorial fashion and to the benefit of the trademark owner, with no intention of infringement of the trademark.

The use in this publication of trade names, trademarks, service marks, and similar terms, even if they are not identified as such, is not to be taken as an expression of opinion as to whether or not they are subject to proprietary rights.

While the advice and information in this book are believed to be true and accurate at the date of publication, neither the authors nor the editors nor the publisher can accept any legal responsibility for any errors or omissions that may be made. The publisher makes no warranty, express or implied, with respect to the material contained herein.

Managing Director, Apress Media LLC: Welmoed Spahr
Acquisitions Editor: Aaron Black
Development Editor: James Markham
Coordinating Editor: Jessica Vakili

Distributed to the book trade worldwide by Springer Science+Business Media New York, 233 Spring Street, 6th Floor, New York, NY 10013. Phone 1-800-SPRINGER, fax (201) 348-4505, e-mail orders-ny@springer-sbm.com, or visit www.springeronline.com. Apress Media, LLC is a California LLC and the sole member (owner) is Springer Science + Business Media Finance Inc (SSBM Finance Inc). SSBM Finance Inc is a Delaware corporation.

For information on translations, please e-mail booktranslations@springernature.com; for reprint, paperback, or audio rights, please e-mail bookpermissions@springernature.com.

Apress titles may be purchased in bulk for academic, corporate, or promotional use. eBook versions and licenses are also available for most titles. For more information, reference our Print and eBook Bulk Sales web page at http://www.apress.com/bulk-sales.

Any source code or other supplementary material referenced by the author in this book is available to readers on GitHub via the book's product page, located at www.apress.com/ 978-1-4842-5835-4. For more detailed information, please visit http://www.apress.com/ source-code.

Printed on acid-free paper

*To Marta, Mikolaj "Nick," Helena, my brother,
and my parents – for your love
To my grandchildren Nessa and Niko
To Raymond Camden, Andrew Trice, Chris Bailey,
and Neil Patterson, without whom we wouldn't dare*

Table of Contents

About the Authors

Marek Sadowski is a full-stack developer advocate, a robotics startup founder, and an entrepreneur. Born in Poland, he has about 20 years of experience in consulting large enterprises in America, Europe, Japan, the Middle East, and Africa. As a graduate from the International Space University, Marek pioneered research on VR goggles for the virtual reality system to control robots on Mars in NASA Ames in 1999. He also founded a startup to deliver robotics solutions and services for industries. In 2014, Marek moved to Silicon Valley to promote Edge, IoT, robotics, and mobile solutions driven with AI, APIs, and Cloud native.

Lennart Frantzell is a developer advocate with IBM in San Francisco, focusing on Blockchain and AI. Born in Sweden, Lennart moved to Silicon Valley in the late 1980s to work with AI technology, especially with Expert Systems. He worked on a team that specialized in taking prototypes from IBM Research and productizing them, making them ready for distribution all over the world. When the "AI Winter" put the brakes to development of Expert Systems, Lennart moved to object-oriented programming and from there to the IBM Internet Division, part of the burgeoning Internet and Web movement in the late 1990s.

About the Technical Reviewer

Matt Rutkowski is an STSM and Master Inventor at IBM developing open infrastructure and industry standards along with open source for over 20 years in areas including banking, digital media and entertainment, and security compliance and specializing in Cloud for the last 9+ years. Most recently, he is the IBM lead for and a committer to the Apache OpenWhisk Serverless computing project at Apache Software Foundation (ASF) serving on its Project Management Committee and as a committer. In addition, he has worked on Cloud Orchestration, Security, Audit, and Compliance standards. Specifically, he has chaired and been lead editor for such standards as OASIS Topology Orchestration for Cloud Applications (TOSCA), OASIS CloudID, and DMTF Cloud Auditing (CADF) which he founded. Furthermore, he has contributed to implementations of these standards within communities such as Apache, CNCF, and OpenStack.

Swift Book Forward

Whenever I present on Serverless computing, I often start by affirming that the name itself is a misnomer and joke some clever marketing person coined it. In retrospect, it is actually a disservice to name such a powerful technology by what it takes away. Granted, I am not going to try to attempt to rename it here nor would I want to try to. Instead, let me suggest that Serverless is best viewed by what it attempts to enable which is allowing programmers to write efficient functions that perform some cool task in their favorite language and not care at all about where it runs or how it scales.

In this book, you will be doing just that, learning how to write Swift language functions that implement some of the most popular use cases that drive adoption of Serverless. These use cases should cause light bulbs to go off as they clearly showcase how turning to Serverless for many common programming tasks can garner large savings in terms of compute costs while reducing operational overhead dramatically. It is my hope that each and every developer who finishes the contents of this book will be able to recognize these patterns when tasked to write some new Cloud-based service and choose to do so using Serverless technology.

Notice that I used the word "attempts" in the first paragraph; allow me to explain. After describing this vision of Serverless and my wishes for you to embrace it, we should have a reality check. Serverless is still trying to figure itself out. What I mean is that despite being generally available in some form as a compute technology offered for more than a few years via services such as AWS Lambda, MS Azure, or IBM Cloud Functions, there is no real standard for how it is implemented. Therefore, the programming and deployment models, the programming conventions, the supported languages, and even the use cases themselves will be presented in different ways (if at all) from different providers. Some Serverless platform providers may not even have a thought-out programming model, a disservice we will discuss, or even include some of the most important features needed to implement the use cases.

Do not despair. In the end, if you write good RESTful functions that are not tightly coupled to proprietary frameworks or APIs, tooling is available to help you easily package them to whichever platform serves your needs the best. The Cloud providers will, in my opinion over time, all evolve to acknowledge the same patterns and strengths and come to support a common programming model based on an event-centric, observer pattern. This book, I am proud to say, chose the Apache OpenWhisk platform which, in my biased opinion, is the gold standard for Serverless. Why do I say that? Because OpenWhisk represents a platform that was originally designed and implemented by many great minds in IBM Research who not only understood the value of creating a highly scalable platform around the observer pattern but also placed the simplicity and usability of the developer as the top priority. After being donated to the Apache Software Foundation (ASF), OpenWhisk only got better as it was battle-hardened and fine-tuned by top-notch developers from around the world. Each of these developers strove to make OpenWhisk code efficient and performant for both their own personal use cases and those of their customers. Even better, they made sure OpenWhisk could be run anywhere and on any Cloud, public, private, or hybrid where you can run containers. Kubernetes became the preferred framework, but experimental deployments have also shown that it could be run on Mesos or OpenShift if needed. I should confess some of my favorite community members actually run OpenWhisk themselves on AWS or IBM Kubernetes services. This is a great way for companies that want to explore hosting their own Serverless platform to test-drive the technology. My colleagues at Apache have even had great success running minimal configurations of the platform for local development or as part of edge computing platforms, which is a nice segue.

What does the future hold for Serverless? When I said that Serverless is trying to "figure itself out," what I more accurately should say is that those who "get it" are running with it. Those that see the goals of event-driven, reactive programming come to fruition without having to stand up even a service framework being realized, now want to take it further. Truthfully, when I think of and talk about Serverless, I mean Function-as-a-Service (FaaS) because in order for the technology to go to places it needs to go to, it needs to be small, fast, and lean. However, so many of us have had to and are still working hard just to migrate legacy applications to Cloud likely using Containers popularized by Docker. Even some of us, excited to adopt Serverless as the ultimate reactive programming platform, have found that we have "bound" great functional code to proprietary service frameworks. In these cases, Containers may be the only simple option to bring our function, whole stack in tow, with us in order to attempt to advantage Serverless scaling characteristics without spending countless hours decoupling code. But never accept that running functions in containers equates to Serverless or is its culmination simply because you can scale them.

As you can imagine with all the code locked in legacy and proprietary frameworks, the reliance and focus on advantaging Containers will go on for quite some time, but Containers are not the end vehicle that will carry Serverless to these new and exciting places. Even as I write this, people in the Apache OpenWhisk community and other cutting-edge visionaries are trying to see how they optimize the best Serverless use cases by taking them "to the edge." Focusing on running simple functions in response to events, what a good Serverless platform does, such as OpenWhisk, aligns well for processing and analyzing data for most modern data needs. This means using Serverless "under the covers" to process event data generated by millions upon millions of Internet of Things (IoT) devices or handle requests to rapidly prepare and serve data to mobile devices as part of Content Delivery Networks (CDNs). Additionally, as you will learn in this book, one of the premier use cases for Serverless is the ability to quickly create APIs in Public Clouds where functions can sniff, modify, or enhance data to and from some existing backend services. If you ever write a new Cloud-based service and do not use Serverless APIs for your frontend, you are likely missing out on many advantages and savings.

In fact, if the programmer-oriented vision I laid out earlier for Serverless holds true, there may be a future where the term "Serverless" evaporates entirely as it just becomes "good Cloud Programming". Swift developers specifically, being highly aware of programming efficiently for mobile and wearable devices, may be the best poised to understand and take Serverless where it needs to go. Indeed, I am quite excited to see an uptick in adoption and discussion of Swift in Serverless circles from the readers of this book to help shape its future.

Cheers to you as you take Serverless for a ride, go "off road," and perhaps take it to see places it has not yet been!

Matt Rutkowski

IBM STSM, CTO for Open Serverless Technologies

June 2020

CHAPTER 1

Introducing Serverless

Today "the Cloud" is everywhere, it permeates our lives, and it is impossible to imagine ourselves without it. Without Cloud technology, we wouldn't have globally available applications like Airbnb, Uber, Facebook, Google, IBM Cloud, Netflix, Apple iTunes, Amazon, and Microsoft Azure, to name but a few Cloud-based services.

Cloud services do not depend on dedicated hardware servers, but on ephemeral APIs[1] that can be accessible by everyone, from anywhere, on any type of device, from desktops to smartphones. All it takes is just a computer, like a lightweight laptop, or even a smartphone.

So the Cloud is really thousands and thousands of APIs coupled to swarms of cheap hardware, and into this revolutionary mix we introduce "Serverless," a new programming model that is changing the world.

Serverless: The next generation of Cloud computing

Serverless has become the new Cloud programming model, which only requires the programmer to pass in the Function-as-a-Service to the Cloud API for execution. It involves no operations or any maintenance for you as a Cloud developer.

---

[1]APIs, a plural of an API – that is a short for an application programming interface – which one would use to access a function of an application.

© Marek Sadowski and Lennart Frantzell 2020
M. Sadowski and L. Frantzell, *Serverless Swift*,
https://doi.org/10.1007/978-1-4842-5836-1_1

Using the Serverless programming model, you can efficiently deploy your APIs with a minimum effort. And serve your APIs without worry while just paying for actual code usage, since the code is being executed by an API consumer.

If you are a client-side developer for iOS in Swift or other mobile or traditional platforms using other programming languages or if you are a Cloud engineer and you want to get hands-on experience in using Serverless – the latest and greatest Cloud-side technology – this book is for you.

Serverless will help you develop lean, Cloud-based APIs that are as cost-efficient and lightweight as possible for consumer and business APIs alike. Serverless technology has been mainstreamed by well-established enterprises like Amazon, Microsoft, Google, and IBM and embraced by startups like Slack and so on where Serverless effortlessly enriches stand-alone applications almost effortlessly with information sourced in Social Networks, results of big data processing, or supported by Artificial Intelligence (AI) and Machine Learning (ML).

If the Cloud became the social and industrial infrastructure of today, then Serverless technology is the latest generation of Cloud services. Serverless services are superlight thanks to dynamical allocation of machine resources. Those resources are allocated only when needed, instead of forcing the developer to pre-arrange these resources ahead of time in order to be used later for the estimated earlier loads. Furthermore, in order to stay on the safe side, the typical server-based resources are often oversized and rarely saturated. While Serverless technology allows operators to adapt and respond to the given load, the provided computers are being billed for only the gigabyte seconds of the allocation that was actually used by the applications. Moreover, organizations that use Serverless are responsible only for the functions they deploy, while Cloud operators are taking care of all the maintenance and operations of the underlying libraries, operating systems, and hardware.

Note   Event-based modern architecture is allowing developers to decrease time to market. This chapter answers the questions what it is, when, why to use it, and how.

Traditional client-server computing has dominated the computer scene since at least the 1980s. Clients connected to beefy dedicated servers, called on-premise (or on-prem servers), which provided the compute and data storage needed for crunching the problems and changing the world. The fall of the Berlin Wall in November 1989 not only proved the superiority of Western democracy but also of the client-server model on which democracy was based.

In the beginning of the third millennium, with newly minted millennials, the Cloud made its entry on the world scene with Amazon's Elastic Compute Cloud. Startup companies realized that they could move their own computer services from their own dedicated data centers to Amazon's Cloud and cut their initial investments and decrease the startup costs dramatically. Instead of paying for hardware upfront, they paid for the access to hardware in time slices.

Servers were cheaper in the Cloud than in each startup's data center, but you still had to pay for maintenance and support on an ongoing basis. What made Serverless revolutionary is that you can now replace monolithic servers with spinning applications on virtual machines (VMs) with Serverless functions. These functions are only invoked by client requests when they are needed. Serverless is a revolution which, going forward, will have repercussions throughout the world. So now the change concerns moving from paying per servers to actual gigabyte seconds the CPUs were spinning for the Serverless functions.

So what is **Serverless** more precisely? Let's consider the following typical scenario for the Serverless function.

A user uploads a picture to her/his Cloud account. As soon as the picture is loaded, it generates an event (the new picture in the folder). As soon as our app detects this event, it triggers a function. The function sends a request to an AI-based Visual Recognition service that tags the pictures. Thanks to provided tags, the app can now update the automatic description and catalogue the picture according to the pre-trained classifiers of Visual Recognition. In such a way, the application may provide a user with suggestions for the image classifications. At the same time, the AI analysis can make the service providers aware if the uploaded content might be Not Suitable for Work (NSFW) due to the explicit or harmful content.

Please see the following simple example implementation of Hello World Serverless function that responds to a simple text input with a simple greeting. As an input, you provide a name in the JSON format:

```
{
    "name": "Marek & Lennart"
}
```

Your Serverless function will respond with the greeting message customized with the provided name. The function itself is written in IBM Cloud in Functions – the IBM implementation of the Apache OpenWhisk project, an open source Serverless platform hosted in IBM Cloud. Since IBM Cloud provides a generous free tier for developers who want to test the examples in this book, they will be based on this flavor of the Open Source project (you might want to use a different provider of Apache OpenWhisk). Your first implementation of a greeting function in Swift will look like this:

```swift
func main(args: [String:Any]) -> [String:Any] {
  if let name = args["name"] as? String {
    return [ "greeting": "Hello \(name)!" ]
  } else {
    return [ "greeting": "Hello stranger!" ]
  }
}
```

This implementation of the Serverless function is authored for the Apache OpenWhisk Swift 4.2 runtime which is hosted as part of the IBM Cloud Functions service running in IBM Cloud. In addition, this function was written in the built-in, language-aware editor that comes with the IBM Cloud Functions user web interface. Figure 1-1 shows how the Swift function looks in the browser.

Figure 1-1. *Serverless function implemented in Apache OpenWhisk as it seen in the IBM Cloud Functions browser-based editor*

When your Serverless function is invoked, the result would look like this:

```
Activation ID:
45a4f1af985e4b93a4f1af985e3b9374
Results:
{
   "greeting": "Hello Marek & Lennart!"
}
Logs:
[]
```

The results will appear on the right-hand side of your editor in a browser (Figure 1-2). You might notice the very short time of the Serverless function execution – especially after the function has been "warmed up" (i.e., called and installed in the memory of the Serverless function engine – we will discuss more on "warming up" functions in the following chapters).

Figure 1-2. *The result of an execution of the Serverless function*

The function was created with the help of the Quickstart Templates of a Hello World function for Swift 4.2 language – please see Figures 1-3 and 1-4 for your reference.

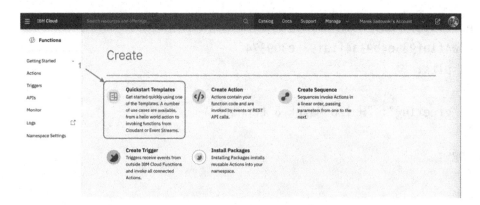

Figure 1-3. *Selecting a Quickstart Templates in IBM Cloud*

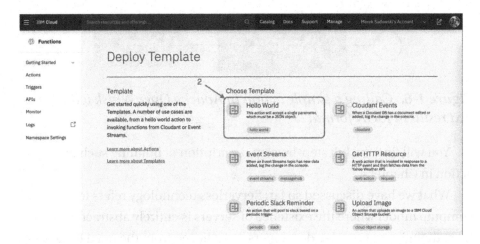

Figure 1-4. *Hello World Serverless template-based example from IBM Cloud*

Finally, the resulting Swift function will appear in your Action library as shown in Figure 1-5.

Figure 1-5. *Hello World Serverless function in the Actions library in IBM Cloud*

The Action here represents the basic executable element of Apache OpenWhisk, which when called produces a result in a JSON text format (Figure 1-6).

Figure 1-6. *Calling a simple action in Apache OpenWhisk with the text result in JSON format*

You will find the full step-by-step description of building such an action in Chapter 4.

What we have discussed so far: Serverless technology refers to a compute model where the existence of servers is entirely abstracted away. Even though servers exist, developers are relieved from the need to care about their operation or the need to worry about low-level infrastructural and operational details such as scalability, high availability, infrastructure security, maintenance, and other details. Serverless computing is essentially about reducing maintenance efforts to allow developers to quickly focus on developing code that adds value and *magically* scales horizontally in the Cloud with the demand. This *magic* is being taken care of and delivered by the Cloud and the Serverless infrastructure providers. In Chapter 2, you will be introduced to leading Cloud providers that offer Serverless technology.

We will use Apache OpenWhisk to run through most of the book and examples. We will cover in great detail Apache OpenWhisk in Chapter 3 of this book. For now, we want you to simply know that we selected the Apache OpenWhisk as it is an open source project – there is not any lock-in to the specific vendor. Apache OpenWhisk works as a distributed Serverless platform that executes functions in response to events at any scale, and it is based on other open source projects. If you are a hard-code developer, you can even run your own Apache OpenWhisk Serverless instance yourself on a Kubernetes cluster or stand-alone in a Java virtual machine on your desktop using the open source instructions.

Apache OpenWhisk manages the infrastructure, servers, and scaling using Docker containers so you can focus on building amazing and efficient applications. Furthermore, Apache OpenWhisk – as a Serverless function flavor – supports Apple Swift language, among other programing languages, and technologies. And this particular feature enabled writing of this book.

Introduction to event-based programming

Amazon Web Services is largely credited with starting the Serverless market hype in 2014 when the company introduced Lambda, its serverless computing product.

General Manager of AWS Strategy Matt Wood said the product was inspired by one of the company's most popular products: Simple Storage Service (S3).

Blogger Sam Kroonenburg says the relationship between S3 and Lambda is an important analogy. "S3 deals in objects for storage. You provide an object and S3 stores it. You don't know how, you don't know where. You don't care. There are no drives to concern yourself with. There's no such thing as disk space... All of this is abstracted away. You cannot over-provision or under-provision storage capacity in S3. It just is," Kroonenburg explains in his A Cloud Guru blog.

Wood says AWS wanted to take that same philosophy to computing. "Lambda deals in functions. You provide function code and Lambda executes it on demand.... You cannot over provision, or under provision execution capacity in Lambda. It just is."[2]

---

[2]www.networkworld.com/article/3187093/serverless-explainer-the-next-generation-of-cloud-infrastructure.html

AWS Lambda[3] lets you run code without provisioning or managing servers. You pay only for the compute time you consume – there is no charge when your code is not running.

With Lambda, you can run code for virtually any type of application or backend service – all with zero administration. Just upload your code and Lambda takes care of everything required to run and scale your code with high availability. You can set up your code to automatically trigger from other AWS services or call it directly from any web or mobile app.

The Apache OpenWhisk follows the idea and concepts started by the Amazon Lambda. Its programming model is shown in Figure 1-7.[4]

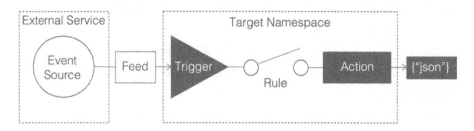

Figure 1-7. *The event-based Apache OpenWhisk programming model*

In response to an event in the external service, a trigger is being activated. Events from various sources might be grouped under the dedicated feeds. The trigger then engages a rule, which selects which action it needs to invoke. Finally, an action is being executed. In some cases, the action might be started in the stated intervals – in the crone-like manner – or called directly from inside of an external service or an app. An action produces a response in the form of a text formatted as JSON. The action can also manipulate other resources with use of the RESTful API calls. That function is described in more detail in the following section.

---

[3]https://aws.amazon.com/lambda/

[4]http://openwhisk.apache.org/documentation.html#documentation

An architecture for Serverless

The typical application will be calling Serverless functions over the API Gateway. API Gateway in this sense groups Serverless functions and might hide some of their features like function-dedicated URLs and so on. Functions then would realize dedicated actions in the SaaS environment. Figure 1-8 demonstrates such an architecture.[5]

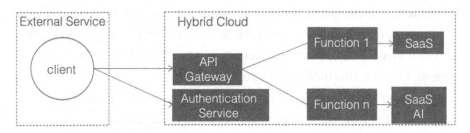

Figure 1-8. *An architecture for a typical Serverless-based system*

In a given Serverless-based system, a client first authenticates with the Authentication Service in the Cloud. Then, by accessing the API Gateway, the client activates functions that realize operations in the Software-as-a-Service (SaaS)-based data systems (DBs, CRMs, ERPs, etc.). There is a close synergy between Serverless functions and SaaS-provided data, since Serverless functions do not store any data on their own. The Serverless functions are stateless. All elements of the Serverless system might be placed in different Clouds, as well as on Premise (in the local data center) systems, yet exposed as an API, in the Dedicated or Private Clouds, as well as in the mix of Clouds from various providers. API Gateway allows for combining single functions (create, read, update, delete) into full CRUD operations, as well as for hiding the source URLs by rewriting them.

---

[5]https://martinfowler.com/articles/serverless.html

In the following sections, you will explore a Cloud-based programming model and benefits of using it. Finally, serverless is relatively new, and we will look at what the shortcomings are with the current technology and how to mitigate them.

Cloud-based programming model

The Cloud native programming model aligns with the evolution of the Cloud infrastructure that was provided to first Business to Business (B2B) and when matured also to single users as a Public Cloud, flexibly and on demand. More on this topic in Chapter 2.

In early 2000 while the existing Cloud infrastructure offered only virtualized hardware, the companies needed to engage the entire IT departments to manage servers. The IT industry used to call this approach as the *Bare Metal* offering or the Infrastructure-as-a-Service (IaaS). Cloud native programming in this case included an approach like with the regular on-premise (on-prem) servers. In IaaS, you have to take care of preparing and uploading the fixes to the hardware even before installing an operating system (OS), patching OS up, there is still a need for the configuration of the networking components, sometimes including the firewalls and their setup. Only then you could possibly start to install the application servers and database engines. Another aspect of IaaS is to connect the required storage servers. Keeping an entire bare metal installation up to date is similar in costs and efforts as to keep your own data center, less the investment in the hardware itself. The so-called value proposition of the bare metal vendors usually was about decreasing Capex (investing and owning the hardware) in favor of Opex (running the operation costs). During the initial Cloud development, the situation was comparable to the discussion at a car dealership, as when you had a need for a car, would you buy it or lease it? Then technology allowed for new options. The programming model here was so traditional. You owned the entire stack, so it has been up to you what kind of application you would run. But you have had to make sure that you could support the entire application installation, new releases, updates to application servers as well as operating systems, the system backups, and even satisfying the requirement of duplicating critical infrastructure. As you could imagine, any change in the system required synchronization among various actors inside and outside of the organization – and therefore it was scheduled only a couple times a year to avoid any outage of the system. I remember being on call or at the customer locations during holiday seasons to facilitate simple updates of the systems, not even the updates of the hosted applications. The monolithic applications, in such an architecture were rarely exchanging information with outside systems, were commonly used in the industry. Message-Oriented Middleware gave some flexibility and connectivity for those core systems. And some features were exposed to early Internet applications.

As soon as the market for virtualizing hardware and offering it in chunks became quite mature, the companies specializing in IaaS started to offer hosting of the virtual machines (VMs). With hosted VMs, the infrastructure became less of a problem for the IT departments (IT). Thanks to the hypervisors responsible for sharing the outsourced hardware platform among various virtual machines (sometimes belonging to various customers), IT was concerned only with installation of the VMs. Each VM consists of the OS, then application servers, and based on it a business application. Still a huge part of the job in a VM environment is to establish the storage elements. Also networking is still an issue, yet more and more taken care of the VM-as-a-Service providers. The VM offering is still more tailored toward B2B customers. The effort to maintain the application in the VM installation is only a fraction of the entire scope. You have to take care of the system administration, its tuning, security hardening, usage authorization, monitoring, and the access control. Only then you can start to contemplate application server administration and finally the business application, tuning the system according to its needs, and respecting the needs of developers. Operations for such a VM-based system is still very time-consuming. The releases are rather on quarterly basis than more often and aligned with the updates or patching of the OS. Everybody in the VM universe follows the waterfall model of delivering applications and its major releases. During first VM adoption, the Service-Oriented Architecture for business applications was ruling in the IT. Systems were assembled into solid blocks that were talking to each other over the Enterprise Service Bus. The Internet 2.0 was born, and applications from various vendors in various places started to connect to each other. Software-as-a-Service was born with the help of SOAP protocol (a messaging protocol specification for exchanging structured information in the implementation of web services in computer networks).[6]

Recently we started to use the Container technology. The arrival of Docker as an open source software that could decrease the time needed to manage an operating system and networking to the minimum, that opened ability to start DevOps practices. Now companies are able to update the application more often, delivering releases quickly, with monthly or even bi-weekly schedules. Companies started to use the Agile method to adapt to market expectations and feedback faster. Startups could start to compete with larger enterprises, mostly taking advantage of the leaner IT, without all the overhead of OS and application server administration. Now everything was containerized. That gave rise to Public Clouds, since now everybody – not only companies – could use Cloud instead of buying their own servers. Despite the fact that companies lost control over the hardware hidden in the Cloud, they gained elasticity in producing the updates and releases more often. Still there was a need for DevOps engineers, who would plan for the rollout of the new releases, making sure there is autoscaling and availability of the containers for their systems. The applications started to be assembled out of microservices, following RESTful API protocol (web services that

---

[6]https://en.wikipedia.org/wiki/SOAP

conform to the REST architectural style, called RESTful web services
(RWS), provide interoperability between computer systems on the
Internet[7]). The systems started to depend on the exposed APIs to SaaS
and specialized in various aspects of technology, from communications,
through customer relationship management, to Social Networks. Now a
microservice became the fundamental element of the provided system.
The rise of the container orchestration technology with Kubernetes as an
Open Source project allowed for the real boom for new systems, while
DevOps engineers could control larger systems with less effort relying
on the automation provided with the Kubernetes technology and release
management offered by following up projects like Istio. The containers
as such are ephemeral, so they require SaaS based stateful systems
to write and read data. Now the releases of particular microservices
started to be scheduled on a weekly basis. Now microservices are living
their independent lifecycle being consumed by various systems in the
microservices economy.

The Cloud providers that expanded their offering from IaaS, thru VMs,
and Containers, started to offer also Platform-as-a-Service (PaaS) – where
already the fully capable application servers are hosted. The example
of such a PaaS platform is IBM Cloud based on Cloud Foundry Open
Source project. Now companies start to deploy only the applications or
microservices. Still customers had to pay for spinning the application
servers with provided CPUs and memory. That gave the space for another
innovation – and the Serverless programming concept was born. Now you
do not need to worry about the management of the servers, the application
server capacity (memory, CPUs, scaling protocols, etc.). In Serverless
programming, everything is going to be taken care of by Cloud providers.
Serverless Functions can't exist without the SaaS stateful systems, but
otherwise the functions can be updated on a daily basis or even more
frequently. And a particular granular function connected with other

---

[7]https://en.wikipedia.org/wiki/Representational_state_transfer

functions – responsible in all, for example, for Creation, Reading, Updates, and Deletion (CRUD) of the resources – becomes a single traditional microservice. You are only responsible for the implementation of a function. If comparing this approach with our buying a car example, the Serverless function is almost like using a car, sharing service by minutes or by hours.

When to use Serverless

Serverless functions are having the best time to market for business functionality. As it is shown in the example in the preceding section, it takes literally a minute to start hosting a Serverless function. In the creation process, there is no need for any capacity or performance planning. These aspects are taken care of by the Cloud provider.

Another aspect of the Serverless Function that is great for any team, or a startup company, is that all the efforts are put in to making the Serverless function better, instead of stealing the time for building the operations model. At the end of the day, being able to utilize Serverless Functions could be the most effective means to minimize application running cost and allow a Serverless provider to attend to all the operational optimization efforts.

Another aspect of leveraging Serverless Functions is the lack of packaging required for your application. In the Serverless function world, the packaging is just the bare minimum, and the application is suitable for running, without or with minimum packaging processes.

Since all the operations are on the Cloud provider side, you do not need to take care of scaling or planning ahead of time to provide the scaling you might need for your Serverless functions – rarely using fully what was booked. The entire process is automatically accommodated by the Serverless platform and the Cloud providers.

Now being able to deploy a Serverless function easily, without engaging larger overhead of IT, you are able to constantly experiment and create new, better versions of your function. You are able to easily implement and deploy new versions that you might leverage for A/B testing. Also it allows you to test your experimental, occasional workloads – you can easily provide some new functionality without requesting a bunch of approvals to deploy such a new functionality.

Finally, Serverless computing is greener computing where you will pay and use only the servers for the time of execution, not the time of their free spinning.

Traditional servers still have their strengths

Whereas Serverless functions are great for light, short-lived, and ephemeral processing, they don't feel right for the processes that are longer, requiring a full transaction capture (like financial or logistics operations).

And since Serverless functions are stateless, the best approach for having stateful tailored services is the traditional approach (serverful) using Platform-as-a-Service (PaaS, for example, Cloud Foundry-based), based on Containers (Red Hat OpenShift, or Kubernetes), or even traditional virtual machine-based systems might be better suited.

Another aspect of generally provided Serverless technology, there is a huge risk of having a vendor lock-in. Therefore, we urge you to consider this characteristic of the Serverless system beforehand, with a list of what-if questions. To mitigate that risk, this book gravitates around Apache OpenWhisk that is an Open Source project supported and developed by esteemed Open Source community, as well by IBM and Adobe, among other industry players.

Also, Serverless functions are susceptible to the "noisy neighbor" problems, since they are often run alongside other functions within servers managed by the Cloud platform provider. You would have well founded concerns for your functions' performance management or traffic steering, since they are still critical to monitor and manage. Also Serverless technology based in the Public Cloud would need to take care of its latency, accidental network shortages, and unexpected performance decreases. To mitigate these aspects, you could opt for the Cloud Private deployments, leveraging projects like Knative eligible for both Private and Public Clouds.

Since the system takes longer for the cold start, some users might experience high latency in their calls. This caveat might be mitigated by keeping a minimum traffic hitting your Serverless functions every couple minutes (some Serverless systems recall the space of unused Serverless services after about 5 minutes of being idle). Or if high QoS is required, it is better to use typical systems based on Containers or PaaS.

Finally, Serverless technology is a new development. There are yet the certifications like HIPAA or SOC to be established for it. At the moment of writing this book, there are scarcely any established tools that support management, monitoring, and operations of your Serverless function-based systems. Therefore, if 99.999% QoS and availability of your system is required or you need fully certified systems (with the HIPAA certification or alike), it is better if you deploy your system on a more mature platform either PaaS-based, a Container-based, or as aforementioned VM- or IaaS-based.

Summary

We hope these cons don't discourage you and still you are ready to experiment and then deploy your first Serverless functions with Apache OpenWhisk technology. The details are demonstrated in the following chapters.

CHAPTER 2

Actors in the Serverless Space

It wouldn't be fair to just jump ahead and start the discussion of Apache OpenWhisk without providing some information about the Serverless technology vendor landscape. This chapter will therefore focus on providing an introduction to the Serverless space, as well as providing arguments for using one or the other Serverless platforms. At the moment of writing, only Apache OpenWhisk supports the Swift language; thus, only IBM Cloud with IBM Cloud Functions is described in the following chapters.

In addition to IBM Cloud Functions, we will briefly describe the other vendors' Serverless implementations, notably Amazon Lambda, Microsoft Functions, Google Functions, and briefly some others.

We will finally describe the economics and reliability of Serverless, the resources required to run Serverless, and the role of the vendor in its operations.

The economics of Serverless

In today's approach to building Cloud-based software systems, achieving the lowest possible execution cost seems to be the primary driving force for large companies and startups alike. The nature of Public Cloud providers allows one to more easily compare various technologies and

© Marek Sadowski and Lennart Frantzell 2020
M. Sadowski and L. Frantzell, *Serverless Swift*,
https://doi.org/10.1007/978-1-4842-5836-1_2

associated runtime costs. Looking at compute services, the closest to actual hardware is Bare Metal with VM-based deployments typically offered as Infrastructure-as-a-Service (IaaS), followed by Container-as-a-Service (CaaS), Platform-as-a-Service (PaaS), and Function-as-a-Service (FaaS or Serverless). PaaS is often implemented using VMs, or Containers themselves, but these details are hidden from the end user. See Figure 2-1.

IaaS	CaaS	PaaS	FaaS/Serverless
Functions	Functions	Functions	Functions
Applications	Applications	Applications	Applications
Runtimes	Runtimes	Runtimes	Runtimes
Operating Systems	Operating Systems	Operating Systems	Operating Systems
Infrastructure	Infrastructure	Infrastructure	Infrastructure

Provided by Developer	Virtualization Provided by Cloud

Figure 2-1. *Comparing the Serverless technology FaaS, CaaS, and PaaS*

Bare Metal and VM-based deployments, even simplified via IaaS abstractions, still are quite costly. They still require large numbers of knowledgeable operators and administrators when deploying and configuring applications. In addition, they require continuous management to apply updates of platform-specific drivers, libraries, and application dependencies. Therefore, we will only seek to compare pros and cons of CaaS, PaaS, and FaaS deployment models in this section.

CaaS or container-based architecture represents a style where you deploy containerized applications on predefined clusters of compute nodes.

CaaS is dominated by Docker-based containers, which are orchestrated by either Kubernetes or Red Hat OpenShift. The deployment style is portable. One can easily move containerized software across various providers, since the majority of vendors support both Kubernetes and Red Hat OpenShift.

Also when compared to FaaS, the largest costs of CaaS are due to cold-start times – that are charged to customers (so-called spin-up). The horizontal scaling is costly, again as each suffers cold start. Furthermore, managing updates to applications, libraries, dependencies, and base images can still take lots of time requiring specialized costly knowledge. Automation of CaaS image builds is not easy and can cause unforeseen churn. The disadvantage of this approach is that you need to take care of spinning up enough containers to manage the workload – thus, you pay for what you do not use. Fortunately, there are plenty of capabilities for autoscaling by increasing and decreasing the number of deployed containers to reflect the demand. Still you are responsible for providing an adequate amount of cluster nodes. The modern style of programing for containers is veering around the microservice mesh rather than the old-fashioned monolith style. Still the containers are ephemeral in their stateless design, requiring Software-as-a-Service (SaaS)-based data storage-oriented systems (databases, CRMs, business core systems, etc.).

PaaS approach is a bridge style between virtual machines (or CaaS) and Serverless, where your application servers are being managed by a Cloud vendor. Often interacting through platform-specific APIs is requiring provider-supported languages or application frameworks and libraries. Think of Microsoft Azure and the required usage of .NET in Azure's management. With PaaS, you are still responsible for sizing the platform specification in terms of instances and memory allocated to the application server instances. There are mechanisms for autoscaling, as well as a plethora of Cloud services to enrich your applications with.

In the PaaS style, you would still deploy your application package using a supported framework such as Kitura, an application server for server-side Swift, that is provided on the IBM PaaS-based Cloud Foundry.[1] In general, as soon as you exceed the free tier in the IBM Cloud, the PaaS approach is more expensive than FaaS, since you need to spin the service up at all times in order to provide the functionality.

Autoscaling in PaaS provides you with some flexibility, but it is also a paid service on its own. Also there is somewhat significant vendor lock-in, due to the PaaS-based service choreography. Thus, portability of applications is still possible, but it is not as easy as with CaaS. See Figure 2-2.

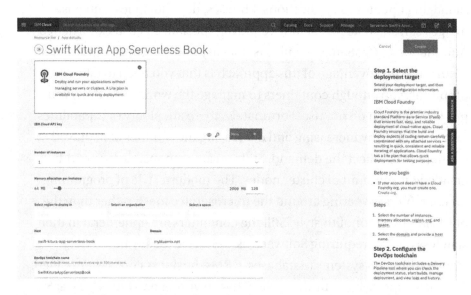

Figure 2-2. *The PaaS-based application service definition for IBM Cloud Foundry-based* `Kitura` *for server-side Swift systems*

---

[1]Open Source Cloud Foundry is the industry standard Platform-as-a-Service (PaaS) that ensures fast, easy, and reliable deployment of Cloud native apps. Cloud Foundry ensures that the build and deploy aspects of coding remain carefully coordinated with any attached services thru VCAP blocks, resulting in quick, consistent, and reliable iterating of applications.

The majority of FaaS vendors offer similar price points using the combined concept of gigabyte seconds which charges you not only on consumed CPU memory but also on time in CPU when running Serverless functions. IBM Cloud Functions, AWS Lambda, Google Functions, Azure Functions, Alibaba Functions, and Oracle Functions offer similar free tiers of about 400,000 GB seconds free of charge usage, majority adding limit of the free request to 1M–2M. However, it should be noted that these providers, regardless of tier, have been actively competing to offer more memory and CPU power to the benefit of the end user.

At the time of writing, Table 2-1 shows the comparable pricing landscape. Also only Apache OpenWhisk supports Swift-based functions. Therefore, we will use IBM Cloud Functions in this book. They offer managed Apache OpenWhisk service with comparable free tier to others of 400,000 GB seconds of Serverless functions execution with the 100 ms step for every 1 ms initiated and the price $0.000017.

Table 2-1. *Comparing the economics of Cloud native technologies*

Vendor	Request	GB Seconds
IBM Cloud Functions	N/A	$0.000017
AWS Lambda	$0.0000002	$0.00001667
Azure Functions	$0.0000002	$0.000016
Google Functions	$0.0000004	$0.0000025
Alibaba Functions	$0.0000002	$0.00001668
Oracle Functions	$0.0000002	$0.00001417

Also you might want to go the "Do It Yourself" route and deploy the Open Source Apache OpenWhisk on your own or IaaS hardware platform. Since the management aspects of the FaaS platform are not the purpose of this book, they are not going to be further discussed here.

The reliability of Serverless

Organizations that are seeking reliable services tend to pay for service-level agreements offering four or five "nines" of availability.

For example, 99.99% of availability means that allowed downtime or unavailability per day is just 8.6 seconds, weekly 1 minute and 0.5 seconds, and monthly 4 minutes and 23.0 seconds. If you compare it to the 99.999% SLA, it means the downtime is limited only to less than 5.26 minutes per year.

Fortunately, not too many systems are requiring overall up time of 99.999% that is so hard to achieve. With Serverless technology, an organization is completely dependent on the infrastructure that is being managed by a vendor.

Note   When you start with Serverless technology and you seek reliability, there is good news for you – IBM Cloud Functions is offering high availability of this Serverless service based on Apache OpenWhisk at 99.99%.

The promise of Serverless technology is that you would abandon the need of the infrastructure control and monitoring when running your Serverless functions. While leveraging a Public Cloud environment, you still should be giving some attention to a problem of the "noisy neighbor" and its impact on your Serverless functions. For example, you might encounter request timeouts, due to a cold start, or network congestion during peak hours. Therefore, you need to prepare adequately for such events as there are still unseen implications of having physical servers and the fiber cables that connect to them, since you cannot typically monitor or manage them directly using higher-level Cloud services like FaaS.

Resources required to run Serverless

A great thing about Serverless is that there are no resources that you need to pay for when your business logic is at rest. So if there is no traffic on your Serverless app, you pay nothing.

Also in the case of singular or rare calls to the business logic, you would save, since your service would generate charges only when being requested.

When the demand for your service grows, you will be paying as you go. But on the other hand with the typical approach, you would have to spin enough servers to provide you the compute power to do the same, or you would hit the compute ceiling and your applications would become unavailable in the peak times. Figure 2-3 provides a great visualization of this concept.

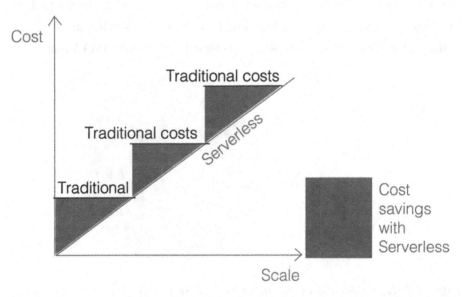

Figure 2-3. *Comparing costs of traditional servers and savings with Serverless pay-as-you-go approach for the growing scale of the demand*

In the serverless space, your application functionality and final efficiency depends on the functionality of the Software-as-a-Service (SaaS). See Figure 2-4. While Serverless functionality or Function-as-a-Service (FaaS) help you with event-based programming, SaaS handles data for FaaS-based functions and stores its data before, during, and after CRUD[2] manipulation. For example, you would get the news article from the Web and analyze it with IBM Watson Natural Language Understanding service. The results you would store for a future use in a CouchDB in the Cloud (offered as SaaS). The preceding business operations you would do with FaaS actions, while reading, analyzing, and storing of reports would be done with the help of SaaS services.

SaaS is responsible for synchronizing data across various Cloud data centers across the world. SaaS can manage any functionality that is responsible for persistent data storing – a traditional SQL database or a modern NoSQL one; it could be a Cloud-based CRM system or a previously mentioned S3-based storage system; eventually, it might be a sophisticated big data processing system, or Machine Learning-as-a-Service, as well as Artificial Intelligence services offered as SaaS like famous IBM Watson.

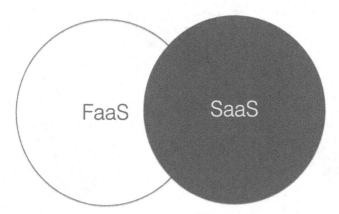

Figure 2-4. *Serverless Functions work closely with Software-as-a-Service (SaaS)*

---

[2]CRUD stands for four operations: Create, Read, Update, and Delete.

Note Serverless Function-as-a-Service depends on the persisting and manipulating of data with the help of the Software-as-a-Service systems. For example FaaS can use SaaS for storing files in S3 capable storage, or for analyzing data with Artificial Inteligence SaaS like IBM Watson.

There is also an option for the FaaS-based system to connect and manipulate data in the on-premise system like a Core Business System (for operations connected with billing, banking, insurances, etc.). In such a case, your FaaS infrastructure might be either hosted for you already in a Private Cloud or you would need to do deploy it for yourself leveraging a framework offered by Knative Open Source project or Red Hat OpenShift to do all the heavy lifting to set up Serverless on top of the container-based infrastructure.

The operation weight is on the Cloud provider side

The Serverless technology is an approach to computing that offloads responsibility for common infrastructure management tasks like provisioning, scaling, scheduling, patching, and provisioning to Cloud providers, allowing engineers to focus their time and effort on the business logic specific to their applications or process.

This leaves developers free to focus on development and also means that you only pay for when your code is running, not when it is sitting idle, which is a huge saving for developers.

Therefore, what matters for you is that your Serverless function is hosted in such a way, that if the current demand for your service requires it, the Serverless platform would scale in an instant from accepting just a couple rare requests for your function to millions of requests during an hour.

All the operations in the Serverless Functions are forced onto the providers – more information on how it has been taken care of by some of them in the following sections.

Since the operation weight for Serverless platform is on the Cloud provider side, for their sake there are limits being introduced. Very often developers underestimate those limits, and thus the applications run into them. The reason for them is obvious one. The vendor needs to make sure that the load remains predictable, so the Cloud resources might be ready to allow for lower latencies and better scaling capabilities. Table 2-2 shows the comparison of the limitations for various key providers.[3]

Table 2-2. *Comparing the limits of Serverless offerings*

Vendor	Memory Max	Execution Max	Payload Max
IBM Cloud Functions	2048MB	10 minutes	5MB
AWS Lambda	3008MB	15 minutes	6MB
Azure Functions	1536MB	10 minutes	no limit
Google Functions	2048MB	9 minutes	10MB
Oracle Functions	1024MB	2 minutes	6MB

The actors in the Serverless space

A sign of how important Serverless has become is the speed with which many mainstream actors, primarily in the Cloud, have established themselves in the Serverless space.

Nowadays every major IT vendor offers the Serverless capability in their Cloud. Let's take a look at the selected IT Cloud providers and their offerings in the following sections.

---

[3]These limitations are as is at the moment of writing of the book; they might change without any notice.

Amazon Lambda

The Amazon FaaS-based platform was introduced in November 2014 to support the Cloud-based business functionality. It premiered right before Black Friday that year, with probably an intent to offer ad hoc compute for merchants during the elevated customer traffic during the high shopping period. The Serverless platform in Amazon is called Lambda and is a part of Amazon Web Services.[4] The disruptive insight that led to Amazon Lambda was that a computing service could be made dramatically cheaper if it was only to run in response to events and automatically managed the computing resources required by those events.

In traditional Cloud computing, if you wanted to run a computing job, you first had to allocate the resources manually and often ended up using more resources than you actually needed.

An example of overuse of computing resources in traditional Cloud computing was to guard against the Christmas Rush and Back Friday, two short events that often forced Cloud-based enterprises to maintain extensive computing resources throughout the year.

Amazon Lambda changed all that and ushered Cloud-based enterprises in the world of "serverless" by not only automatically allocating resources, when they were needed, but also de-allocating them, when they were no longer used. All that was done without human intervention. It has become a true revolution in Cloud computing.

In the original goal, it was to handle smaller and on-demand applications. Those applications were triggered in a response to events and new information. AWS attempts to launch a Lambda instance within milliseconds when there is an event.

AWS Lambda set the philosophy of running a code without provisioning or managing servers, a task you hand over to the backend logic. The following languages were supported at that time: Java, Go,

---

[4]Amazon Lambda: https://aws.amazon.com/lambda/

PowerShell, Node.js, C#, Python, and Ruby. Lambda also provides a runtime API which allows you to use any additional programming languages to author your functions.

With Lambda, you can run code for virtually any type of application or backend service – all with zero administration. Just upload your code and Lambda takes care of everything required to run and scale your code with high availability. You can set up your code to be automatically triggered from other AWS services or call it directly from any web or mobile app.

Lambda provides resource-level control of each application, enabling you to publicly share applications with everyone or privately share them with specific AWS accounts. To share an application you've built, publish it to the AWS Serverless Application Repository.

As the first out of the gate and with its well-known focus on usability and ease of use, Amazon Lambda is a powerful player in the serverless play and a good vendor to turn to get started learning Serverless.

Microsoft Azure Functions

Generally if you develop primarily in .Net-based ecosystem, you would turn to Microsoft Azure Functions for the Serverless technology. Azure had initially offered serverless functions as "web jobs" which evolved and got rebranded as it supported more use cases in response to Lambda. Azure Functions platform was launched in 2016 in response to AWS Lambda. Like AWS Lambda, Azure Functions is a serverless compute service that enables you to run code on demand without having to explicitly provision or manage infrastructure. Azure offers lower pricing for Microsoft Windows and Microsoft SQL, so if you are a Microsoft shop and your language of choice is C# or F# while leveraging Azure resources, probably the easiest choice would be Azure Serverless technology.

Besides Microsoft has done a good job to make it easy for developers to quickly get up and running on Azure Functions by providing hands-on tutorial examples, like the following:

1. Create a Cognitive Services API Resource.

2. Create a function that categorizes tweet sentiment.

3. Create a logic app that connects to Twitter.

4. Add sentiment detection to the logic app.

5. Connect the logic app to the function.

6. Send an email based on the response from the function.

The Twitter app is a very good entry point for using Azure Functions. You begin by creating a connection to your Twitter account. The logic app then polls for tweets, which trigger the app to run, and it can take action depending on what tweets contain.

Azure Functions obviously focuses on Microsoft's base of languages and supports C#, F#, Node.js, Python, PHP, Bash, Batch, and PowerShell.

Google Cloud Functions

Google released its solution in 2016. Google Cloud Functions, or GCF for short, used to lag behind both Azure Functions and AWS Lambda but in 2018 recovered and improved greatly.

Like two others, the Google Cloud Functions is a serverless execution environment for building and connecting Cloud services. With Cloud Functions, you write simple, single-purpose functions that are attached to events emitted from your Cloud infrastructure and services. Your function is triggered when an event being watched is fired.

Google Cloud Functions can be written in Node.js, Python, and Go; and executed in language-specific runtimes. The Cloud Functions execution environment varies by your chosen runtime.

Google Cloud Functions can be consumed by developers through the Cloud Console and Cloud SDK. Also command-line interface gcloud can be used to manage functions.

Google provided the Cloud Functions Framework that allows it to run and test the Serverless code locally first, before deploying it to the Cloud. Yet it is available as a NPM module, so it supports only Node.js deployments.

As Kelsey Hightower, a Google developer advocate, put it during the podcast interview at *Command Line Heroes Episode 5*[5] "At the end of the day, as a developer, you really just want to just kind of check your code in and expect that code to land in front of your customers somehow, someway."

IBM Cloud Functions

If IBM Watson is the technology you want to consume in your Serverless functions, probably the easiest way to do it is with IBM Cloud Functions. IBM launched its Serverless platform quietly in 2016. It provides you with less lock-in by design thanks to its managed Open Source Serverless project – Apache OpenWhisk. If needed, you can be deploying Apache OpenWhisk on premise or in another Cloud with Red Hat OpenShift.

Based on Apache OpenWhisk, IBM Cloud Functions is a polyglot FaaS programming platform for developing lightweight code that scales automatically and executes on demand.

---

[5]www.redhat.com/en/command-line-heroes/season-1/the-containers-derby

IBM Cloud Functions provides access to the Apache OpenWhisk ecosystem in which anyone can contribute their action code as building blocks to the expanding repository.

This book gravitates around Serverless Swift. And at the moment, only Apache OpenWhisk provides out-of-box, runtime support for versions of Swift Serverless functions. IBM Cloud Functions is likely the largest managed Serverless service based on Apache OpenWhisk available in every major region around the world. Therefore, we are going to have a deeper discussion of its capabilities and inner workings.

With IBM Cloud Functions, you can use your favorite programming language to write lightweight code that runs app logic in a scalable way. You can run code on demand with HTTP-based API requests from applications or run code in response to IBM Cloud services and third-party events.

IBM Cloud Functions currently provides support for many language runtimes such as Node.js, Java, Python, PHP, and Swift. Furthermore, you can easily add any language or escape the limitations by integrating any programming language by using a Software Development Kit (SDK) to upload your own language runtimes as Docker containers. As you grasp the technique of containerizing your applications, you would be able to use any language with IBM Cloud Functions. And as with other platforms, you can focus on writing app logic instead of worrying about autoscaling, high availability, updates, or maintenance. IBM provides the underlying hardware, networking, software administration, load balancing, and plug-ins along with complete operational oversight. You just have to bring the code for your functions.

Also which we are going to demonstrate in this book, IBM Cloud Functions offers a catalog of templates in Swift language and other languages to help you get started on your next project. Templates are a combination of actions, triggers, and sequences. Some templates also incorporate other services from IBM Cloud. By using these templates, you can understand how IBM Cloud Functions entities work together and even use these entities as a basis for your own project.

Furthermore, the action code runs when it is directly invoked by the Cloud Functions API, command-line interface (*CLI*), or Cloud Function iOS Software Development Kit (SDK).[6]

Open Source and Serverless

There is always an option for organizations using Serverless technology to Do It Yourself (also known as "DIY"). There are a couple reasons for going "DIY" at least. Since the vendors introduced limits in order to cope and manage the Serverless workloads, the rise of a plethora of Open Source projects came into life to overcome these challenges of managed Serverless platforms. For example, organizations might bump into the limits of a payload or the memory allocation of Serverless functions.

These frameworks include Apache OpenWhisk (Apache License), OpenFaaS (MIT license), Kubeless (Apache License), Knative (Apache License), the FN Project (Apache License), and Fission (Apache License), among others. Their aim is to allow you to deploy and manage your own Serverless platform without the limitations imposed by vendors discussed in the previous sections.

Apache OpenWhisk offers one of the solutions for escaping the limits on the size or technology – going with containerized Serverless actions using Docker. But be aware that at the same time you are going to lose the peace of mind, and you are after the task of managing the clusters and scaling for your Serverless platform.

---

[6]The iOS SDk is no longer actively supported and no official released versions are published. The repos are provided "as is."

If starting your own operations and associated costs is worth waving the limits imposed on the Serverless platforms offered by vendors, you need to answer that yourself.

It is worth mentioning that some of these frameworks are already being used by some major vendors. For example, Apache OpenWhisk is offered as an IBM Cloud Functions and Adobe is using it "under the covers" for Adobe I/O. Additionally, a fork of the Fn project is the technology behind Oracle Functions.

Apache OpenWhisk

Apache OpenWhisk is an open source, distributed Serverless platform that executes functions (fx) in response to events at any scale. OpenWhisk manages the infrastructure, servers, and scaling using Docker containers so you can focus on building amazing and efficient applications. One of the important achievements of this Open Source project is its official graduation to become an Apache Software Foundation (ASF) Top-Level Project in July 2019.

In late November 2016, OpenWhisk was accepted to the Apache Incubator by IBM donations of its beta-level code from IBM Research. Before this acceptance, the codebase was being used by IBM customers as the underlying technology for IBM Cloud Functions.

The OpenWhisk platform supports a programming model in which developers write functional logic in any supported programming language that can be dynamically scheduled and run in response to associated events from external sources or from HTTP requests. The project includes a REST API-based command-line interface (CLI) along with other tooling to support packaging, catalog services, and many popular container deployment options.

Since Apache OpenWhisk allows for native use of Swift for defining and running Serverless functions, we will explore how to author Swift functions in the next section and use them to create compelling Serverless applications in the following chapters.

Summary

This chapter provided you with an introduction to the Serverless space and gave you arguments for using one or the other Serverless platforms. In this book the authors described in detail the managed Apache OpenWhisk in IBM Cloud known as IBM Cloud Functions. Nevertheless, you have been introduced briefly here also to other vendors' Serverless implementations, notably Amazon Lambda, Microsoft Functions, and Google Functions. Finally, the economics and reliability of Serverless was shown, in addition to the resources required to run Serverless and the role of the vendor in its operations.

CHAPTER 3

Apache OpenWhisk – Open Source Project

Marek speaking: "Most of my 20+ year IT career has been with server-side Java. It started with Sun Microsystems' Java when it was a new language used mostly in web page applets in 1995-97. Back in 1996 I started my Java adventure by writing one of the first server-side Java systems creating Web Forums dedicated to the Disaster Recovery in NTT in Japan. Since then plenty of new and old systems were built or migrated to server-side Java and eventually to the cloud.

We believe that the same development is happening now with the Apple Swift programming language. It was released at Apple's 2014 Worldwide Developers Conference (WWDC). Since then it has been adopted by various application servers, Cloud native development, and Serverless technology. There are advantages to using server-side Swift in plenty of fields. And now you can have a career as a full-stack developer using Serverless Swift for cloud-native programming."

For starters, you can easily pick up Serverless Swift or server-side Swift if you already are familiar with iOS client development. By extending your skills to the serverless or server-side, you can become a full-stack developer. Thus, based on the authors' experience, adding Serverless skills is really critical in one's career development. Or simply starting with Serverless Swift and this book, you can become an expert at Cloud native development with Cloud based Swift.

© Marek Sadowski and Lennart Frantzell 2020
M. Sadowski and L. Frantzell, *Serverless Swift*,
https://doi.org/10.1007/978-1-4842-5836-1_3

It is also beneficial for companies to use the same language and code constructs on the mobile client, as well as in Serverless and/or on the server-side. Using a single language on a client, on the server, and in the Cloud increases the readability of code, its maintenance, and further development.

Taking some of these advantages into account, when we were asked to write about the Serverless Swift, we instantly jumped at the task, believing it to be an outstanding opportunity to share our career experiences with a broader audience. We are also strong believers in the power of Open Sourcing a modern and mature language such as Swift. This chapter will explain what happened behind the curtains during the conception of Apache OpenWhisk. We hope that adopting it will allow you to expand your own professional career.

In the following sections, you will find in-depth information about Apache OpenWhisk as an open source project and who the main promoters of the project are. We will also discuss Swift becoming fashionable with its Open Sourcing allowing you to bring your skills from native device development (iOS and macOS alike) to the Cloud. We will finally use this opportunity to provide some advice on when to use it and when it might be an antipattern.

Overview of Apache OpenWhisk Open Source project

In early 2015, a small group of IBM Researchers launched a new effort under the name of *Whisk*, in order to allow programmers to move quickly and nimbly. Whisk, which soon became *OpenWhisk*, was envisioned as a

Cloud-first and distributed event-based programming incubator project at IBM Watson Research Center in New York.[1]

---

whisk/(h)wisk/ (a verb) – take or move (someone or something) in a particular direction suddenly and quickly.

The project's initial idea was to allow code to be executed, and the committed resources to the program were whisked away after execution. The project name was lent to the command-line interface (CLI) that was named **wsk**, also spelled *"whisk" after it*. The prefix *Open* was added at the later stage to accent *Open Sourcing* of the Whisk project.

The incubation project got traction and was soon developed into a full research project. IBM announced the project in 2016 in Las Vegas during the IBM InterConnect conference.

Analysts were excited to learn about the OpenWhisk's features and that the project was open sourced under the Apache 2 license. Also from that early start, the technology became generally available to IBM customers via IBM Cloud. There is a significance in this, since the same source code, which IBM had already beta-tested, and that was used to commence the project at Apache, was already considered by IBM as production ready and provided to IBM's customers.

The IBM Research team developed the majority of the core programming model and the runtime system that is in use today. As the code was donated to the Apache Software Foundation and OpenWhisk became a part of an Apache Incubator and was being developed further with a growing list of contributors, including developers from Adobe and Red Hat, among many others. Today Apache OpenWhisk is an open source, distributed serverless platform that executes functions in response

---

[1]https://researcher.watson.ibm.com/researcher/view_group_subpage.php?id=9368

to events. OpenWhisk manages the infrastructure, servers, and scaling using Docker containers, so you as a developer can focus on building applications.

Note   Since *OpenWhisk* is a part of the Apache stack, anyone can join the project and become a contributor. And as a contributor to the Apache ecosystem, developers can redefine their own career development as Open Source contributors and programmers.

Since the OpenWhisk announcement in 2016 and along with AWS Lambda and Google Cloud Functions, the platform offered another option for those interested in event-based programming and Serverless architectures. The Apache community has developed it to be a resilient, highly scalable, production-quality platform, with approved Apache governance. As an Open Source project, it has also become recognized as the most comprehensive, enterprise ready, proven Serverless platform solution. At the time of writing, Apache OpenWhisk has almost 900 forks and more than 4600 stars in its GitHub repository with various development tools.

The big milestone for the Apache OpenWhisk community happened in 2019, when the platform officially graduated and became the Apache Software Foundation's ***Top-Level Project***.[2]

The Apache's Top-Level Projects are those with healthy Open Source communities and active development, with numerous technology and project listings.

The downstream community (further from the original upstream community) pushed for innovations and included development for Edge FaaS computing, allowing its codebase to be run even on Raspberry Pi computers.

---

[2]https://developer.ibm.com/technologies/serverless/blogs/
apache-openwhisk-community-graduation/

The project currently supports numerous languages and includes among others the following additional features:

- Command-line interface ("wsk" CLI)

- API clients for multiple languages

- OpenWhisk Composer for functional composition

- The package deployment tool

Please find the current up-to-date components in Figure 3-1.

Apache OpenWhisk Components

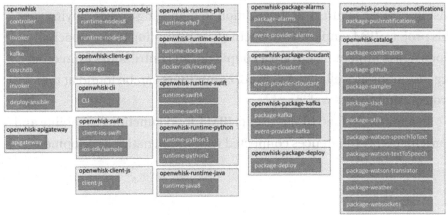

Figure 3-1. *Apache OpenWhisk Components*

The areas of focus for the future development include the work on Knative, Tekton CI/CD pipelines, and Kubernetes event-driven autoscaling (KEDA). Also new use cases to add new protocols, finer-grained access control to functions using proxies like Envoy.

Who is supporting the Apache OpenWhisk project?

The Apache OpenWhisk is a popular project, and it is being used by companies as a managed solution in the following Cloud offerings: IBM Cloud, Adobe I/O, Nimbella, and others. In addition, it is a part of other solutions, like the Knative project, or available thru Red Hat OpenShift.

Apache OpenWhisk laid the foundation for IBM Cloud Functions back in 2016 as IBM donated the project of its research. And still today IBM is providing Apache OpenWhisk service as its managed version on IBM Cloud in order to offer the Serverless technology to IBM Cloud customers (see Figure 3-2). In addition to managing and deploying this project, IBM employees are actively contributing to the Apache OpenWhisk project. There are a couple dozen contributors from other organizations as well. The full list of committers can be found at the project committers' web page.[3]

In addition to that, IBM presents IBM Cloud Functions capability and participates in conferences connected with Cloud native development.

---

[3]https://projects.apache.org/committee.html?openwhisk

Figure 3-2. *The screenshot of the IBM Cloud Functions welcome web page*

But IBM is not the only supporter of the Apache OpenWhisk project. There are other organizations that contribute, promote, and help businesses to deploy applications using Serverless actions. Among these companies, you can find the following (see the attached screenshot from early 2020): Adobe, Abilisense, AdvisorConnect, Altoros, Articoolo, BigVu, CloudStation, GreenQ, IBM, NASA JPL, KONG, Magentiq Eye, Naver, NeuroApplied, Nimbella, QZCloud, Red Hat, SiteSpirit, and WSO2; see Figure 3-3 for the list of supporters.

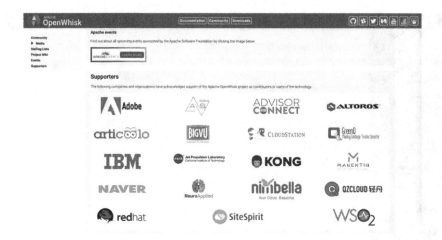

Figure 3-3. *The screenshot of the list of supporters of Apache OpenWhisk project*

In addition to IBM, there are also others who offer managed Apache OpenWhisk in the Cloud. Among those, Adobe is also providing managed Apache OpenWhisk on their Cloud Adobe I/O (see Figure 3-4).

Figure 3-4. *Adobe I/O Cloud with Apache OpenWhisk as the Serverless engine*

Interesting approach to managing and expanding the Apache OpenWhisk has been taken by Nimbella (see Figure 3-5). They are offering stateful features for Serverless technology.

Figure 3-5. *Nimbella offers stateful features for managed Serverless Apache OpenWhisk platform*

Natively supported languages by Apache OpenWhisk

Apache OpenWhisk supports a growing list of your favorite languages such as NodeJS, Go, Java, Scala, PHP, Python, Ruby, Swift, Ballerina, .NET, and Rust.

You might want to use other particular languages that are not supported out of the box. There is a solution for that as well: you can create and customize your own executables as Zip Actions. In order to run them, you need to use Docker SDK to run them on the Docker runtime. There are complete tutorials for using Docker Actions for Rust and Haskell.

The big advantage of writing Serverless actions in a language you use on the client is that you can reuse the same constructs both on the client side and on the Cloud side. It improves the clarity of the code and decreases the number of used technologies. Now you can program in your language of choice both on the client and with Serverless technologies.

The Swift language is one of the most important native languages supported by Apache OpenWhisk. The language is relatively young, but with a huge and rapidly growing usage base.

The adoption of Swift as an open source language

The evolution of the Swift language is quite similar to Java back in 1996. It took 10 years from the first public implementation of Java 1.0 in 1995 to the almost complete release of the Java virtual machine as free and open source under the terms of GNU General Public License. Much quicker approach was made by Apple with promotion and release of Swift, which was announced by Apple during WWDC in 2014, and was made open source with Apache 2 license on December 3, 2015, with Swift version 2.2.

Since the new language for the entire Apple ecosystem became a big hit, and surprise, it started to become one of the fastest growing in popularity programming languages along JavaScript, Python, and C#.

Seeing the opportunity to capitalize on the server-side aspect of the Swift, IBM as one of the first adopters of Swift started to strategically position and promote server-side solutions for this new language. IBM promoted Kitura – a Swift-based free and open source web framework. The Kitura framework was soon available on IBM Cloud (see Figure 3-6).

Figure 3-6. *Kitura as the open source web framework is offering Swift on the server-side*

Others didn't stay behind. There is Vapor, also a very popular web framework based on an open source Swift, that released version 1.0 as a proof of concept for Swift on the server-side. The source code for Vapor is hosted on GitHub, under MIT license.

Initially, Swift started to be seen as the fastest growing language among top 10 programming languages, but fell behind the first 10 languages and has stayed in the top 20 since 2018.

With growing interest in Serverless Swift and business applications using server-side Swift with Kitura and Vapor, it might again climb to the top 10 languages.

Server-side vs. Serverless

But what is the difference between the server-side and Serverless Swift? When should you use one or another? That is a very valid question for the enterprise architecture, and you need to approach it with caution.

The server-side solution

First, there are two major server-side Swift Web frameworks – Vapor and Kitura. Vapor is being developed by the community, eager to implement the latest and greatest of the Swift features, but often breaking backward compatibility in the process, while Kitura has been mostly promoted by IBM contributors. And because of its enterprise angle and in order to maintain the rock-solid performance and stability, Kitura has stayed backward compatible and has always been thoroughly tested when introducing new revisions.

Secondly and frankly speaking, at the time of the writing of this book, both platforms are still lacking in maturity, so you might be a pioneer when taking the server-side Swift path. You might be ending by writing missing frameworks for yourself.

You should ask yourself some typical architectural questions as well as organizational ones:

Do you have enough system administrators to manage a highly available (HA) infrastructure?

When Marek was an IT architect supporting development of systems in large financial institutions in years 2006–2009, the traditional approach was the only one available. And Marek with the team would not stop at the idea of HA. Also, they would approach the challenge of the recovery centers in physically different locations. Since then, an experienced IT architect realizes that there is a need for quite the skilled and experienced operations team for managing such HA infrastructure with the geographically separated recovery center.

Does your project have a budget for spinning up extra server capacity in order to handle a transaction peak during hot seasons like Black Friday or Winter/Summer Holiday Sales? If needed, can you scale your applications fast enough, in order to respond to higher demand in peak times? Are you ready to monitor your application resilience and deal with costs of running at least two processes for high availability for your system? Do you want to monitor these running processes for their health? Have you thought about deployments in different regions?

You must consider the costs of such HA infrastructure, since you are going to be charged always, even if idling, while having on average about 20% usage of the platform that is dedicated to your application. In addition, your traditional system often might be continuously polling other systems to simply check if there are any required actions to be taken. This is due to lacking an event programming model. Also relaying on Platform-as-a-Service and Container Orchestration is deemed to be less efficient than Serverless from the operations point of view. And when scaling up, you would be paying for coarse-grained scale-ups for reserved resources based on time to meet demand. See Figure 3-7 for Vapor as the traditional application server based on server-side Swift.

Figure 3-7. *Vapor along with Kitura offers the open source web framework for the server-side Swift*

Finally, you need to make sure that your Cloud components need to run over longer periods of time, which can be mostly done only with the traditional approach.

The Serverless solution

On other hand when deciding to go with the Serverless technology, are you able to be satisfied with 99.99% of availability of your system? Can you accept cold starts – or does your application need to be more responsive?

It is better to picture Serverless technology as one without server operations on the part of the developer or their organization. You deploy your business logic, and you do not need to worry about provisioning of servers, clusters, and the management of the underlying infrastructure.

Moreover, with the Serverless technology based on Apache OpenWhisk, the execution model creates the code snippets into a runtime

SDK to execute, and pause, waiting for further requests for about 5 minutes. There is one process per request, so it scales inherently. From the very start, your microservices would be based on the event-based programming model. The Serverless platform helps developers to build well-designed, Cloud native microservices easier, offloading many of the operational best practices recommended by the 12-factor[4] app.

Since you are not going to host long-running processes that need HA or multi-region deployments, there is no cost associated with upfront resilience.

To summarize, when using Serverless, you are charged only for what you use. So, as a developer, you need to worry only about your code. You can achieve higher development velocity, while you lower operational costs. This is particularly true with application scaling, container lifecycle management, and workload concurrency, especially difficult when the modern system is based fully on the microservices. Therefore, Serverless platforms can start to address some of those operational concerns.

If you either revise some part of the legacy system that is built in the traditional way or you expand it, you might want to consider using Serverless as the Cloud Native Approach while you also gradually adapt the Cloud. Also, when you start with a new development, Serverless seems the ideal choice as it is highly cost-effective and much simpler from the DevOps point of view.

Extending iOS programming with Serverless in the Cloud

One of the best reasons to start with Serverless is when one is already an iOS developer who wants to learn server-side or Serverless access to the backends. The IBM Cloud Functions provides you with a Software

---

[4]https://12factor.net

Development Kit for iOS – iOS SDK – that allows you to seamlessly connect with the Serverless tier and execute instantly Serverless Actions in the Cloud, almost like you would be doing them locally on the device.

There are a couple integration points to be specified, but other than that, you are just calling another library. With that integration, you can start your journey with Serverless. These are the parameters you need to provide in order to leverage iOS SDK:

- The Cloud Foundry-based `namespace` to connect to Serverless Functions

- The OpenWhisk `Package`

- The OpenWhisk `AppKey` – associated with the namespace

- The OpenWhisk `AppSecret` – associated with the namespace

- And finally the name of your Serverless action

All these details are included in the example `OpenWhiskIOSStarterApp`. Then using your favorite dependency manager either CocoaPods or Carthage, you will be able to add additional needed libraries (see Figure 3-8 for details).

Figure 3-8. *IBM Cloud Functions provides the iOS SDK for fast implementation of the Mobile Serverless Backend-as-a-Service*

As many mobile applications require server-side logic, curated access to Social Networks, or extension with Machine Learning or AI services, Serverless is one of the best technologies to leverage on demand. And since a client-side developer usually might not have experience in managing infrastructure, it will be much easier to let the operations part be taken care of by the Cloud provider and just use directly the managed version of Apache OpenWhisk.

It is the same language and you are able to use the same native style of coding in Swift and the same libraries both on the client and in the Cloud in Serverless Actions.

When to use Serverless – and when not – patterns and antipatterns

A good practice is to use Serverless for a new feature or functionality, especially when you build a new system from scratch. Serverless is also suitable for small teams.

Yet, due to its infancy of the language, it is not recommended for large IT projects or for replacing an existing legacy application. The recommended route is to containerize a legacy system, rather than migrate everything to the serverless.

When you want to develop a Serverless-based system, follow these suggestions:

- The function logic is state0

- less.

- Functions are idempotent.

- There is just one task per function.

- Functions should finish as quickly as possible.

- Recursion can be avoided.

- You need to be aware of the concurrency and rate limits.

Here come some **patterns** that fit the Serverless approach:

- Consuming simple APIs via HTTP requests. Providing that functions stay stateless, you can cache the sessions and subscribe to the event channel, so they get the messages with new events.

- Fanning out the tasks into subtasks, and when the task has completed, fanning in the results from individual workers. You need to consider exceeding the limits of the Serverless platform.

- Using API Gateway as a proxy to encapsulated atomic Serverless functions, called idempotent, that you could constantly update with constant releases.

- Performing the gateway aggregation with the Serverless function decreasing the communication overhead between a client and the backend.

- Publish-subscribe services using messages to inform each other about events happening in the environment and reacting to each other.

- Queue-based load leveling, where, for example, a queue helps you to decouple tasks from services for less responsive systems; this makes it possible to reduce spikes or to obtain response from various systems with very different response times in a response queue. But you must avoid synchronous calls at all costs.

- The strangler pattern where the Serverless action is a dispatcher of requests between a legacy system and new features built with the Serverless framework.

- Read-intensive calls – like the most popular hashtags – can be cached in dedicated views. When you ask for the hashtag, you get access very quickly. But you need to watch out for handling of the cache, since it is a sophisticated task that adds cost, and additional business logic into system.

- For processing streams and pipelines from IoT sensors or web UI clickstreams.

Knowing the patterns for diving into the Serverless Actions is a great start for your building a Serverless system. But you must avoid using the one tool for all your challenges.

The term antipattern was coined by Andrew Koenig: "An antipattern is just like a pattern, except that instead of a solution it gives something that looks superficially like a solution but isn't one."

Therefore, you should analyze the following **antipatterns**:

- Prepare for cold starts, because your client would suffer the wait time while you load dependencies. Do not treat your Serverless actions as server-side code full of unnecessary dependencies – like classes in the dependency tree at the startup – since you would pay by warming the Serverless container.

- Do not ignore the logging resources to trace problems in your Serverless actions. You should consider adding correlation ID across invocations of APIs to nail down faulty code.

- There are already code patterns for typical code uses for Serverless technologies. Instead of doing everything from scratch, look for existing patterns that might already address your business problem.

- You should still be using naming conventions for functions since not doing so might result in code that is very hard to maintain.

- Despite running a Serverless project without "hardware" or "operations" in mind, you shouldn't drop the best practices of source control, code reviews, and static analysis of the code. Also you should add unit tests and execute them at build time, since there is a huge value in unit testing.

- Do not go the way of recursion – you might get the bill you don't want to ever see. This is a big no for all event-driven models.

- You might discuss using Serverless technology to rebuild an entire system. The rule of thumb in such a situation is to at most tackle just a small part of such a system or its new functionality. Avoid replacing what is stable and working.

Summary

This chapter discussed the OpenWhisk project, its conception, and current development. You have also discovered traditional server-based projects in Swift. Therefore, you got some information when to use serverless, which patterns to implement, and which one to avoid. With the information about Apache OpenWhisk under your belt, now is the time to create your first *"Hello World"* Serverless action!

CHAPTER 4

Hello World from Apache OpenWhisk in Swift

After completing this chapter, you will be able to code and run your first serverless actions in a Cloud using the Swift programming language from both a browser-based editor and a command-line interface (CLI). Once the action is created, you will be able to invoke the action's function from a mobile iOS application.

"Hello World"

Let's begin by coding what developers typically call the "Hello World" program to accomplish the task of making our Swift Serverless function respond with the simple string: `"Hello World"`. In the case of Serverless actions, the actual response from the Cloud will be in JSON (JavaScript Object Notation)-formatted text:

```
{"message" : "Hello World"}
```

And this response will arrive very quickly thanks to the direct use of Cloud-based programming tools and services, which many call Cloud native programming.

© Marek Sadowski and Lennart Frantzell 2020
M. Sadowski and L. Frantzell, *Serverless Swift*,
https://doi.org/10.1007/978-1-4842-5836-1_4

Writing the first Hello World in Swift

Your first Cloud function will be written in a web browser in the provided web user interface of IBM Cloud, where you can find the free tier for using managed Apache OpenWhisk as Function-as-a-Service offering, FaaS for short. In order to access IBM Cloud, first you need to sign up for a free Lite account. Then after confirming your email, you are ready to type and test your first Cloud functions.

Start simply by visiting this page:

`https://bit.ly/serverless-swift-cloud-account`

which will redirect you to IBM Cloud signup page, and you would proceed through several steps described in details in Appendix A in order to claim your free IBM Cloud account (also known as the Lite account).

From now on when you visit the IBM Cloud using this link `https://cloud.ibm.com,` you should be able to see the Dashboard. From the "hamburger" menu button (see Figure 4-1), select the IBM "Functions" entry to navigate to IBM Cloud Functions web user interface (see #1 in Figure 4-2). The details on using the IBM Cloud Functions are specified in Chapter 5 and some navigation in Appendix A.

Figure 4-1. *Expand the top-left navigation menu (also known as a "hamburger") with a click*

Select the "Start Creating" button (#2 in Figure 4-2) and choose Quickstart Templates in the next screen (#3 in Figure 4-3).

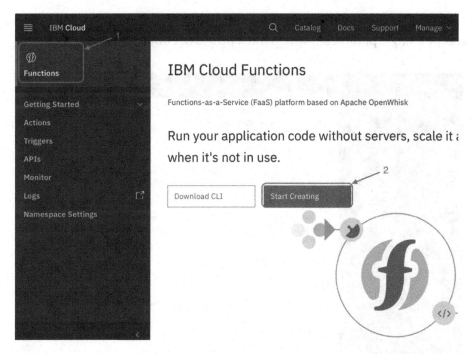

Figure 4-2. *"Start Creating" your first IBM Cloud Functions with a template*

This will lead you to a set of various templates where you will then select the "Hello World" template (#4 in Figure 4-4).

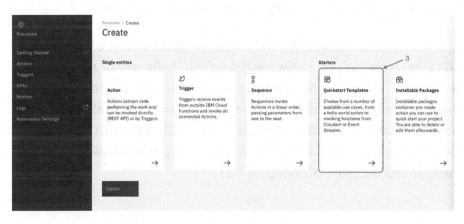

Figure 4-3. *Select "Quickstart Templates"*

By default, the action made from the "Hello World" template will accept a single parameter, which must be a JSON object.

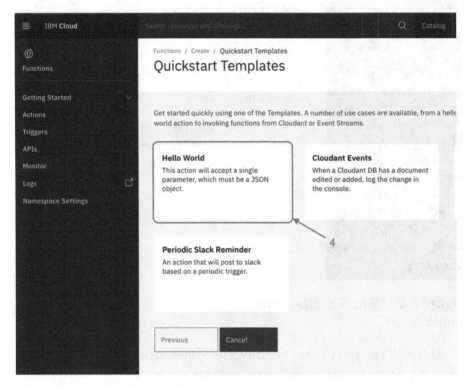

Figure 4-4. *Choose the "Hello World" quickstart template*

At this point, you can enter a Package Name, for example, `serverless-swift-hello-world`, or simply use the default "hello-world" one already provided (#1 in Figure 4-5). Then you need to select the desired runtime language from the drop-down list; in this case, your options should include the latest versions for Node.js, Python, PHP, or Swift. Of course, you want to choose Swift (#2 in Figure 4-5). Now you can deploy the action based on this template (#3 in Figure 4-5).

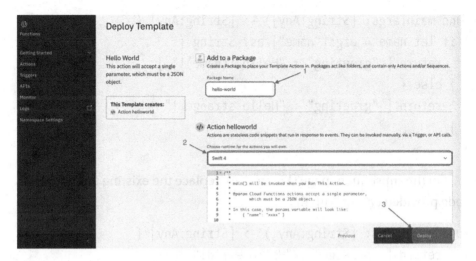

Figure 4-5. *Select "Swift 4" from the runtime drop-down list*

You will see a spinning circle, and after a moment, your action will be ready. In the edit window, you will see the default "Hello world" function code displayed:

```
/**
 *
 * main() will be invoked when you Run This Action.
 *
 * @param Cloud Functions actions accept a single parameter,
 *         which must be a JSON object.
 *
 * In this case, the params variable will look like:
 *     { "name": "xxxx" }
 *
 * @return which must be a JSON object.
 *         It will be the output of this action.
 *
 */
```

```swift
func main(args: [String:Any]) -> [String:Any] {
  if let name = args["name"] as? String {
    return [ "greeting" : "Hello \(name)!" ]
  } else {
    return [ "greeting" : "Hello stranger!" ]
  }
}
```

On the subsequent page (Figure 4-6), replace the existing template code provided earlier with this:

```swift
func main(args: [String:Any]) -> [String:Any] {
    return [ "message" : "Hello World!" ]
}
```

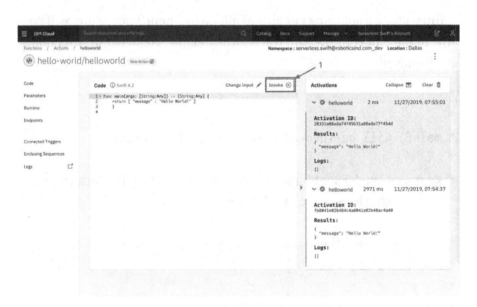

Figure 4-6. Edit, save, and invoke your IBM Cloud Functions

Now, after pressing "Save," you are ready to run your first action by pressing the "Invoke" button (#1 in Figure 4-6). As soon as you invoke the action for the first time, the function is going to be provisioned in the Cloud, as you receive a status message back in the "Activations" window:

```
Action running for ... (timeout 60 sec)
Activation ID:
e99df9edece449b29df9edece439b2dd
Results:
No results yet.
Logs:
No logs yet.
```

Each time you invoke your action, an Activation record is created with a unique ID that can be used to track information about the action's execution including runtime including results and logs.

This first request was considered a "cold start." **The cold start** of a program means that this is the first call of a program which has not yet been loaded into memory. And because of this, it usually takes an additional 2–3 seconds for the first call to a function to respond. In addition, you also need to add the time for the Apache OpenWhisk container defined for your Swift language stack to be provisioned.

After only a short while for the provisioning of the container and starting your function, the activation information will be updated with the awaited response "Hello World" in the JSON form:

```
helloworld
2824 ms 11/2/2019, 21:23:06
```

```
Activation ID:
e99df9edece449b29df9edece439b2dd
```
Results:
```
{
  "message": "Hello World!"
}
```
```
Logs:
[]
```

If you press "invoke" a second time, you will see now that another activation with a new ID will appear in the window this time with a much shorter invocation time. This is because the code is now provisioned or "warm" and will remain so for a period of time for your account type (e.g., on the order of several minutes).

Congratulations! This was your first IBM Cloud Functions and a Serverless action running directly from a browser!

If you invoke the action again, you will see another activation appear with a new ID will appear in the window this time with a much shorter invocation time.

This is because the code is now provisioned or "warm" and will remain so for a period of time for your account type (e.g., on the order of several minutes). Specifically, the action is processed on an already provisioned container in IBM Cloud making it 10–100 times faster than when doing the same from the cold start.

Simple actions like "Hello world" are supposed to take less than 10 ms to execute. In the following results, the code execution time was only 2 milliseconds:

```
helloworld
2 ms 11/2/2019, 21:24:03
```

```
Activation ID:
90e1655a7fa74520a1655a7fa7652072
Results:
{
  "message": "Hello World!"
}
Logs:
[]
```

Actions can execute longer-running code, but keep in mind that IBM Cloud imposes limits[1] for things like maximum execution time depending on your account type. In addition, your function can be de-provisioned after being idle for 5 minutes, after which you will experience the same "cold-start" time you saw initially.

Note   Take into consideration and mitigate against cold-start times when designing your application using Serverless functions. Typically, this is not a problem for most applications since the overhead is relatively small compared to network routing times.

You will find more on the warmed up functions in Chapter 5 and perhaps how you might be able to influence the cold-start response times and keep your function "warm."

---

[1]The current limits are shown here: https://cloud.ibm.com/docs/openwhisk?topic=cloud-functions-limits

Create a Hello World from a command-line interface

In this section, you will create a "Hello World" action for IBM Cloud Functions using a command-line interface, CLI for short. Before you begin with writing and invoking your action from a terminal window, you need to get the prerequisites – the command-line interface working from inside your terminal window (Figure 4-7).

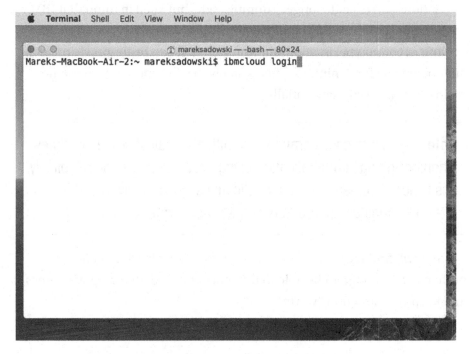

Figure 4-7. *A terminal window in Apple macOS*

Setting up the local environment

In order to create a serverless function in IBM Cloud from the CLI in a terminal, follow the steps shown under CLI submenu of the IBM Cloud ➤ Functions ➤ Getting Started menu. Check Figure 4-2 for your reference and look for *CLI* – command-line interface – under "Getting Started" submenu. You will need to download the IBM Cloud CLI and then install IBM Cloud Functions plug-in.

Note   IBM Cloud Functions uses Apache OpenWhisk "under the covers" which uses the **wsk** CLI command for managing actions; however, it is preferable to use the supported **fn** command (supplied by the IBM Cloud Functions plug-in) with the IBM Cloud going forward although the **wsk** command is still available as an alias for **fn** in the Cloud Functions plug-in for compatibility.

The following steps show how you can begin to use the IBM Cloud Functions CLI plug-in to interact with Cloud Functions entities. According to IBM Cloud documentation, you should be able to use the stand-alone Apache OpenWhisk CLI since all of the command options and arguments for commands in the Cloud Functions CLI plug-in are the same as the options for the OpenWhisk stand-alone CLI with some differences.

However, the Cloud Functions plug-in is preferred since the OpenWhisk CLI may not always have the latest features supported by Cloud Functions, such as built-in awareness of IAM-based namespaces, automatic security token refresh, and advanced API security features. Additionally, The IBM Cloud Functions plug-in automatically utilizes your current login and target information to maintain your client-side configuration and access tokens for all services.

Step 1. Download and install the IBM Cloud CLI.

From the IBM Cloud Functions web user interface, you can begin by selecting the "CLI" menu option under "Getting Started" menu (see #2 in Figure 4-8) and follow their instructions to "Download IBM Cloud CLI" (#3 in Figure 4-8). This link takes you to a full set of installation instructions which primarily have you use your browser to access the official ibm-cloud-cli-releases GitHub repository here:

69

https://github.com/IBM-Cloud/ibm-cloud-cli-release/releases/
where you will need to download the appropriate CLI build for your
desktop operating system and hardware architecture.

Figure 4-8. *Installing IBM Cloud CLI from the IBM Cloud Functions
user interface*

Step 2. Log in to IBM Cloud from a terminal using ibmcloud CLI.

After you installed the CLI, you are ready to use it with IBM Cloud. Log
in to IBM Cloud using the just installed command-line prompt as shown in
the following steps. It will look similar to this:

```
$ ibmcloud login -a cloud.ibm.com -o "serverless.swift@
roboticsind.com" -s "dev"
```

Step 3. Install IBM Cloud Functions plug-in.

When you are connected to IBM Cloud, you can now install IBM
Cloud Functions plug-in, which is based on Apache OpenWhisk, into the
ibmcloud CLI using the following command:

```
$ ibmcloud plugin install cloud-functions
```

You should see the successful result of the installation of the plug-in:

```
Plug-in 'cloud-functions 1.0.36' was successfully installed
into /Users/<your-username>/.bluemix/plugins/cloud-functions.
Use 'ibmcloud plugin show cloud-functions' to show its details.
```

Step 4. Point to the resource group.

Now you need to target the right resource group. You can always check what resource groups there are:

```
$ ibmcloud resource groups
```

```
Retrieving all resource groups under account Serverless Swift's
Account as serverless.swift@roboticsind.com...
OK
Name      ID                 Default Group   State
Default   <some id>          true            ACTIVE
```

Now you can choose the adequate resource group:

```
$ ibmcloud target -g Default
```

Step 5. You have set up your local environment.

And finally, now you can list all the functions:

```
$ ibmcloud fn list
```

You should see output similar to the following one:

```
Entities in namespace: default²
packages
/serverless.swift@roboticsind.com_dev/hello-world-serverless-
swift-cli private
actions
```

---

²IAM and CloudFoundry-based namespaces are discussed in Chapter 5.

/serverless.swift@roboticsind.com_dev/hello-world-serverless-
swift-cli/helloworld private swift:4.2
triggers
rules

That "ibmcloud fn list" command's output proves that your local environment is set up correctly. You are ready to start to use CLI in the terminal.

Writing your Hello World in the terminal

Now it is time to write your function in the terminal. For that, you will start with cloning the GitHub[3] repository of the function templates:

```
$ git clone https://github.com/serverless-swift/helloworld-cli.git
```

```
$ cd helloworld-cli/
```

Now change the code of your helloworld function in the following file actions/helloworld.swift using your favorite editor:

```
func main(args: [String:Any]) -> [String:Any] {
  return [ "message" : "Hello World!" ]
}
```

For example, you could use VIM editor on macOS – this works on the majority of the Linux and Unix systems too:

```
$ vim actions/helloworld.swift
```

---

[3]For cloning a repository from GitHub, you need to use its CLI – git – download and install it from the official repository: https://git-scm.com/downloads; alternatively without the git CLI, you can simply download a zip file from https://github.com/serverless-swift/helloworld-cli and extract it in the target directory.

With VI or VIM in order to insert and change the code of the file, use "i" as for "insert", and when you are done editing, use the following combination to exit and write the file: Esc key and then ":wq" (colon ":" and command "w" like in "write" and "q" like in "quit") as shown in Figure 4-9, and then hit the "return" key (if you want to abandon changes, just type ":q!" to exit editing without saving changes).

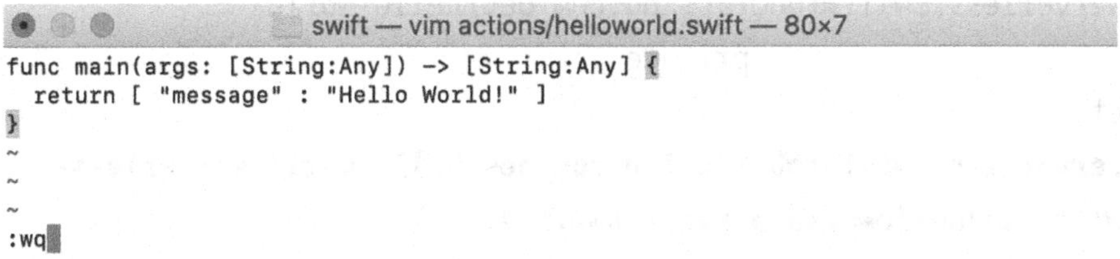

```
● ◌ ●                    swift — vim actions/helloworld.swift — 80×7
func main(args: [String:Any]) -> [String:Any] {
  return [ "message" : "Hello World!" ]
}
~
~
~
:wq
```

Figure 4-9. *Editing* helloworld.swift *function in a terminal with VIM*

Deploying the function in IBM Cloud

Let's deploy the code of our function to IBM Cloud:

```
$ PACKAGE_NAME=hello-world-serverless-swift-cli ibmcloud fn
deploy -m manifest.yaml
```

You will get the following output:

Success: Deployment completed successfully.

You can list all functions with the following command:

```
$ ibmcloud fn list
```

And you should find the new package and your function created from CLI in a terminal:

```
Entities in namespace: default
packages
/serverless.swift@roboticsind.com_dev/hello-world-serverless-
swift-cli private
/serverless.swift@roboticsind.com_dev/hello-world
                        private
actions
/serverless.swift@roboticsind.com_dev/hello-world-serverless-
swift-cli/helloworld private swift:4.2
/serverless.swift@roboticsind.com_dev/hello-world/helloworld
            private swift:4.2
triggers
rules
```

In addition, you can also find your function in the IBM Cloud Functions dashboard – see Figure 4-10.

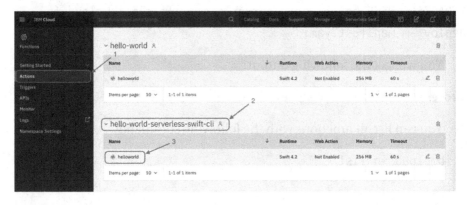

Figure 4-10. *helloworld action as seen in the IBM Cloud Functions dashboard*

Calling your action from a terminal

Now you are ready to test the action. Run the following command in a terminal:

```
$ ibmcloud fn action invoke --result hello-world-serverless-
swift-cli/helloworld
```

You should get the following response after waiting a short time allowing for cold-start provisioning:

```
{
    "message": "Hello World!"
}
```

Congratulations! This was your first action running from CLI in a terminal! You might also want to update your action if you change the code. In order to do it, use this command:

```
$ ibmcloud fn action update hello-world-serverless-swift-cli/
helloworld actions/helloworld.swift
```

You will see the following confirmation:

```
ok: updated action hello-world-serverless-swift-cli/helloworld
```

Calling a Serverless function from a mobile iOS app in Swift

As soon as your serverless action from the previous section is working, you can call it from within a mobile app. In general, creating a business logic in a Cloud – outside your mobile app – gives you the ability to enrich your app by incorporation of APIs and allows you to reach out to Social Networks and connect with other users. With Serverless technology, you can now create a Serverless Mobile Backend-as-a-Service, also known as MBaaS, and it might be all written in Swift. In order to do it, you need to obtain and pass a token to your Serverless namespace associated with IBM Cloud Functions, and you are able to call it from your iOS app, and other applications virtually from anywhere provided access to the Internet. This section will show you how to connect an example iOS app with the IBM Cloud Function. And since IBM Cloud Functions provides the iOS Software Development Kit (SDK) in their web user interface, the steps shown here help you quickly to connect your first iOS app with your "Hello World" function.

The development process in this section requires that you use the Apple operating system (OS) called macOS Catalina 10.15.1 or newer and the Apple integrated development environment (IDE) Xcode 11.2.1 or newer.[4] You will also need to use CocoaPods as the open source free package manager which can be installed from `https://cocoapods.org/`.

Note   If you are not sure that you have the CocoaPods package manager, run the command $ `pod --version`, and if there is an error or you haven't installed CocoaPods, install it now with the following command: $ `sudo gem install cocoapods`.

Assuming that you have the aforementioned development environment installed and ready, you are good to use the following steps to connect your first iOS application with the Serverless functions.

Step 1. Download the example iOS app.

This section provides you with the simple iOS app – please use the following book GitHub repository to clone it:[5]

---

[4]IDE and OS are made available free of charge on Apple computers.

[5]Alternatively, you can simply download the zip file from `https://github.com/serverless-swift/helloworld-ios`

```
$ git clone https://github.com/serverless-swift/helloworld-ios.
git
```

And after it fully cloned, change the directory to helloworld-ios:

```
$ cd helloworld-ios/
```

Step 2. Use CocoaPods to download dependencies.

Run the following command to install the dependencies with the CocoaPod package manager:

```
$ pod install
```

The resulting output should be something like this:

```
Analyzing dependencies
Pre-downloading: `OpenWhisk` from `https://github.com/apache/
incubator-openwhisk-client-swift.git`, tag `0.3.0`
Downloading dependencies
Installing OpenWhisk (0.3.0)
Generating Pods project
Integrating client project

[!] Please close any current Xcode sessions and use
`OpenWhiskStarterApp.xcworkspace` for this project from now on.
Pod installation complete! There is 1 dependency from the
Podfile and 1 total pod installed.
```

Now you are ready to open the project in Xcode, using the workspace file named OpenWhiskStarterApp.xcworkspace (which CocoaPods created for you).

Step 3. Set up your iOS app in the iOS SDK within Cloud Functions.

Within the "Functions" menu of the IBM Cloud user interface, select "iOS SDK" under the "Getting Started" menu (see #1 in Figure 4-11).

Figure 4-11. *IBM Cloud Functions iOS SDK selection*

If you have never created an iOS before in Cloud Functions, you will be asked to select a Cloud Foundry (CF)-based namespace to logically host your packages and functions. You will see a screen similar to one shown in Figure 4-12. Open the drop-down near the top to see all your IAM and CF-based namespaces and select a CF-based namespace (see #2 in Figure 4-12).

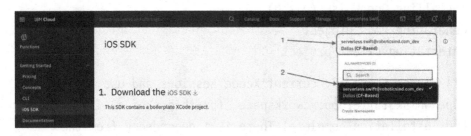

Figure 4-12. *IBM Cloud Functions iOS SDK selection*

Now you can copy over the WhiskAppKey and the WhiskAppSecret that you will use in the mobile app (see Figure 4-13).

Figure 4-13. *Copying WhiskAppKey and WhiskAppSecret*

If you do not have a valid CF-based namespace or you have already used IBM Cloud with an IAM-based namespace, you might see a screen similar to one shown in Figure 4-14.

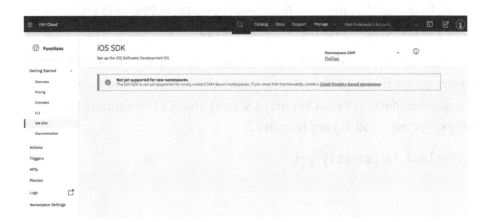

Figure 4-14. *iOS SDK at the moment of writing this book only supports CF namespaces*

Simply follow the instructions to create a CF-based namespace and then select it from the drop-down.

Step 4. Update your iOS "Hello World" app, with the IBM Cloud authorization values shown for your account.

Once you have selected a CF-based namespace, you will see a set of instructions to download and install the iOS development kit and use the "starter app" provided which we already completed in Step 1.

What we care about are the values displayed for WhiskAppKey and WhiskAppSecret from the page (highlighted as #1 in Figure 4-13) which are needed to access your IBM Cloud Functions action from your application.

Update the following constant values in the ViewController.swift file in Xcode (see #1 in Figure 4-15) with the values displayed above in the IBM Cloud Functions user interface along with the namespace name selected in Step 2:

```
let WhiskAppKey = "some key"
let WhiskAppSecret = "some secret"
let MyNamespace: String = "Namespace ID"
let MyPackage: String? = "hello-world-serverless-swift-cli"
let MyWhiskAction: String = "helloworld"
```

Alternatively, you may find your default "whisk namespace" (id) (again, assure that is CF-based) and your "whisk auth" authorization string (i.e., a combination of your key and a secret) from CLI by running the following command in your terminal:[6]

```
$ ibmcloud fn property get
```

---

[6]Remember to maintain the logged in session in IBM Cloud – you can follow the initial steps shown in the previous sections "Create a Hello World from a command-line Interface" and "Setting up the local environment" – Steps 2, 4, and 5.

This command should return something similar to the following example:

```
whisk API host          us-south.functions.cloud.ibm.com
whisk auth              <some key>:<some secret>
whisk namespace
serverless.swift@roboticsind.com_dev
client cert
Client key
whisk API version       v1
whisk CLI version       2019-11-12T22:04:48+00:00
whisk API build         2019-11-20T16:55:46Z
whisk API build number  whisk-build-13199
```

Interestingly, these values were also used to create and invoke the "Hello World" function using the IBM Cloud CLI in the previous section. The IBM Cloud CLI and Cloud Functions plug-in automatically configured these values for you when using the CLI, but they can be used by other clients, such as the iOS SDK, to target namespaces and authenticate to the IBM Cloud.

Step 4. Run your app in the simulator.

Now you are ready to run your Hello World iOS app in the simulator in Xcode integrated development environment on your macOS. First, specify the version of the simulator – see #2 in Figure 4-15 – for example, choose iPhone 11, and select the start button shown as #3 in Figure 4-15. After a moment, a simulator will appear with the start screen. You can hit "Tap me" in the simulator (#4 in Figure 4-15), and it will launch a Serverless MBaaS and provide you with the response from your Serverless function (#5 in Figure 4-15).

Figure 4-15. *helloworld action as seen in the IBM Cloud Functions dashboard*

Summary

Congratulations! You have run your first Serverless action from a mobile iOS app as MBaaS! In the next chapters, you will learn various ways of building Serverless actions, as well as methods to trigger them. You will also learn how to build warmed up Swift actions to cut down their Cloud provision time to avoid the cold start.

CHAPTER 5

Apache OpenWhisk Deep Dive

This chapter introduces main development concepts of Serverless technology with Apache OpenWhisk. After completing it, you will have a good notion of various techniques being used in building Serverless applications. You will find more details on *functions*, *rules*, *triggers*, event *providers*, iOS SDK, *entities*, *namespaces*, *permissions*, and *sequences* that are ready for you in IBM Cloud Functions – the managed Apache OpenWhisk platform.

Marek says: "As it happens I am a scuba diver. When you get introduced to scuba diving you learn the basics of submerging yourself in open waters. There is an equivalent of "Hello World" in diving - an Intro to Diving - where you effortlessly get with a divemaster to explore shallow waters near the shore. Then, if you start to like diving, you want to learn the basics and attempt to get the Open Water scuba diving license. This allows you to explore the general Open Water diving sites within recreational depth limits. As your taste and desires to explore deeper situated wrecks and sites grows you want even more to expand your knowledge and go deeper. You need to test for the Deep Dive license, that allows you to understand techniques for exploring the greater depths, their dangers and diver's recreational limits. I am personally always excited to get the next deep dives." This chapter allows you to get ready for the next level and start coding a real-life Serverless application in the next chapter. Let's take this deep dive into Serverless right away.

© Marek Sadowski and Lennart Frantzell 2020
M. Sadowski and L. Frantzell, *Serverless Swift*,
https://doi.org/10.1007/978-1-4842-5836-1_5

Functions

As you already know from previous chapters, the Apache OpenWhisk Serverless actions, also called Cloud Functions in the IBM Cloud ecosystem, let you focus on writing code and building great solutions, without the hassle of setting up, configuring, or maintaining servers. You will pay only for what you use and not the idle time. And the IBM Cloud allows you to not worry about the demand, since it meets 99.99% availability of your Functions, indifferently if they are being called once a day, or when there are thousands of parallel requests per second.

With them you can run code for any type of application or backend service, all with zero administration.

Note   OpenWhisk actions can be invoked directly via the REST client or indirectly by external events which are sometimes made easier via provider services that act as event proxies. Regardless, one need never worry about "lock-in" as all these are provided as part of the Apache open source.

The *function*, when invoked, accepts as input a JSON dictionary of key-value pairs and by default is expected to produce a JSON dictionary of paired values as output. The dictionaries are canonically represented as JSON objects when interfacing to an action via the REST API or the CLI.

Packages

In OpenWhisk, you can use packages to bundle together a set of related actions and share them with others. Entities do not have to be contained in a package, but as your actions increase in number, you will want to use them to avoid name collisions.

A package can include *actions* and *feeds*, but not triggers and rules:

- **An action** is a piece of code that runs on OpenWhisk.
  For example, the `Cloudant` *package* includes *actions* to
  read and write records to a Cloudant database.

- **A feed** is a special action used to configure an external
  event source to fire *trigger* events and has a special
  interface to manage its lifecycle. For example, the
  `Alarm` *package* includes a *feed* that can fire a *trigger* at a
  specified frequency of incoming messages.

Package nesting is not allowed; this means that you cannot group
packages into another *package*.

An *organization + space* pair corresponds to an OpenWhisk
namespace. For example, the organization `ServerlessSwift@`
`roboticsind.com` and space dev would correspond to the OpenWhisk
namespace `/ServerlessSwift@roboticsind.com_dev`.

You can create your own *namespaces* if you're entitled to do so.
The `/whisk.system` *namespace* is reserved for public packages that are
distributed with the OpenWhisk system.

Every OpenWhisk entity, including *packages*, belongs in a *namespace*.
If a namespace is not specified when creating an entity, the system places
it under a default namespace for the account. A fully qualified name of an
entity takes the following form:

`/namespaceName[/packageName]/entityName.`

Notice that the forward slash character "/" is used to delimit
namespace, package, and *entity names within the fully qualified name.*

For convenience, when developers reference an entity in the default
namespace, the *namespace* can be left out.

For example, consider a user whose default namespace[1] is
/ServerlessSwift@roboticsind.com_dev.[2] The following are examples of
the fully qualified names of a number of entities and their aliases:

- /whisk.system/cloudant/read – The *namespace* is
  /whisk.system, the package cloudant, and the entity
  read.

- /ServerlessSwift@roboticsind.com_dev/filter –
  The *namespace* is /ServerlessSwift@roboticsind.
  com_dev, the *alias* is filter, and the *entity's* name is
  filter.

- /ServerlessSwift@roboticsind.com_dev/video/
  transcode – The alias is video/transcode; the
  namespace is /ServerlessSwift@roboticsind.
  com_dev, the *package* is video, and the *entity's name* is
  transcode.

The following sections describe how to browse packages and use the
triggers and feeds in them.

Browsing *packages*

Several *packages* are registered with OpenWhisk. You can get a
list of *packages* in a *namespace*, list the *entities* in a *package*, and get a
description of the individual *entities* in a *package*.

---

[1]Developers can set the default namespace in their properties file (and override
  the one placed there when the CLI/client was installed and configured).
[2]IAM namespaces would look different.

> **Note**   To start working with the command-line interface, connect first to IBM Cloud and the IBM Cloud Functions following the instructions from Chapter 3, section "Setting up the local environment" Steps 1–5 (Steps 1 and 3 should have been already done; if not, you can start with them now). The "ibmcloud fn list" command's output proves that your local environment is set up correctly and you are ready to start to use CLI in the terminal.

1. Get a list of *packages* in the /whisk.system *namespace*.

    Run the following command in the terminal:

    ```
    $ ibmcloud fn package list /whisk.system
    ```

    The command's output should be similar to the following:

    packages
    ```
    /whisk.system/cloudant                 shared
    /whisk.system/slack                    shared
    /whisk.system/utils                    shared
    /whisk.system/samples                  shared
    /whisk.system/websocket                shared
    /whisk.system/weather                  shared
    /whisk.system/cos                      shared
    /whisk.system/messaging                shared
    /whisk.system/alarms                   shared
    /whisk.system/pushnotifications        shared
    /whisk.system/watson-textToSpeech      shared
    /whisk.system/github                   shared
    /whisk.system/combinators              shared
    /whisk.system/watson-speechToText      shared
    /whisk.system/watson-translator        shared
    ```

The command returned a list of packages in the public
/whisk.system *namespace* that are available for all developers.

2. Get a list of *entities* in the /whisk.system/cloudant
package.

Run the following command in the terminal to find out all the
entities in the package:

```
$ ibmcloud fn package get --summary /whisk.system/
cloudant
```

The command's output should be similar to the following:

package /whisk.system/cloudant: Cloudant database
service   (**parameters**: *apihost, *bluemixServiceName,
dbname, host, iamApiKey, iamUrl, overwrite, password,
username)
...
 action /whisk.system/cloudant/write: Write document in
database   (**parameters**: dbname, doc)
 action /whisk.system/cloudant/read-document: Read
document from database   (**parameters**: dbname, docid,
params)
 action /whisk.system/cloudant/read: Read document from
database   (**parameters**: dbname, id, params)
...
action /whisk.system/cloudant/read-updates-feed:
Read updates feed from Cloudant account (non-
continuous)   (**parameters**: dbname, params)
feed   /whisk.system/cloudant/changes: Database change
feed   (**parameters**: dbname, filter, iamApiKey, iamUrl,
query_params)

Note   *Parameters* listed under the package with a prefix * are predefined, bound *parameters. Parameters* without a * are those listed under the annotations for each *entity.* Any entity listed under a *package* inherits specific bound *parameters* from the *package.* To view the list of known *parameters* of an entity belonging to a *package,* you will need to run a get --summary for that individual *entity* which we will show as follows.

This output shows that the Cloudant package provides the actions read and write and the *trigger* feed called changes. The changes feed causes *triggers* to be fired when documents are added to the specified Cloudant database.

The Cloudant package also defines the parameters username, password, host, and dbname. These parameters must be specified for the *actions* and *feeds* to be meaningful. The *parameters* allow the *actions* to operate on a specific Cloudant account, for example.

3. Get a description of the /whisk.system/cloudant/ read *action.*

   Run the following command in the terminal to see the details of the specific action:

   ```
   $ ibmcloud fn action get --summary /whisk.system/
   cloudant/read
   ```

The command's output should be similar to this:

```
action /whisk.system/cloudant/read: Read document from
database
(parameters: *apihost, *bluemixServiceName, dbname,
*id, params)
```

Notice that the parameters listed for the *action* read were expanded upon from the *action* summary compared to the *package* summary earlier. To see the official bound *parameters* for *actions* and *triggers* listed under *packages*, run an individual get `--summary` for the particular *entity*.

Note   This output shows that the Cloudant read *action* lists five *parameters*, three of which are predefined. These include the document ID to retrieve.

Invoking actions in a package

You can invoke actions in a package, just as with other actions. The next few steps show how to invoke the `greeting` action in the `/whisk.system/samples` package with different parameters:

1. Get a description of the `/whisk.system/samples/greeting` action.

   Let's run the following command to get the details of the action:

   ```
   ibmcloud fn action get --summary /whisk.system/samples/
   greeting
   ```

So as we see in the following details, the *action* / `whisk.system/samples/greeting` returns the greeting.

```
action /whisk.system/samples/greeting: Returns a
friendly greeting (parameters: name, place)
```

Let's test it without and with two parameters: `name` and `place`.

2. Invoke the action without any parameters.

    First, let's invoke the action without parameters:

    ```
    ibmcloud fn action invoke --result /whisk.system/
    samples/greeting
    ```

    As the result of the *action,* the following JSON is returned with the default values for the name and place parameters:

    ```
    {
        "payload": "Hello, stranger from somewhere!"
    }
    ```

3. Invoke the action with parameters.

    Now, let's pass values to the function's two parameters, the name "Lennart" and the place "Silicon Valley":

    ```
    ibmcloud fn action invoke --result /whisk.
    system/samples/greeting --param name Lennart
    --param place "Silicon Valley"
    ```

The results are as follows:

```
{
    "payload": "Hello, Lennart from Silicon Valley!"
}
```

The output JSON used the name and place
parameter values that were passed to the *action* on
the invoke command.

Creating and using *package* bindings

It is not always convenient to use the *entities* in a *package* directly alike
in the previous sections, since you might find yourself passing the same
parameters to the action every time. In order to avoid such repetitions, you
can bind the default *parameters* to a package. These parameters then will
be inherited by the *actions* in the *package*.

For example, in the /whisk.system/cloudant *package*, you can set
default username, password, and dbname values in a *package* binding, and
these values are automatically passed to any *actions* in the *package*.

In the following simple example, you bind *parameters* to the /whisk.
system/samples *package*:

1. Bind to the /whisk.system/samples package and
    set a default place parameter value:

    ```
    $ ibmcloud fn package bind /whisk.system/samples
    ServerlessSwiftSamples --param place "San Francisco"
    ok: created binding ServerlessSwiftSamples
    ```

2. Get a description of the *package* binding:

    ```
    $ ibmcloud fn package get --summary
    ServerlessSwiftSamples
    ```

package /serverless.swift@roboticsind.com_dev/
ServerlessSwiftSamples: Returns a result based on
parameter place
   (**parameters**: *place)
 action /serverless.swift@roboticsind.com_dev/
ServerlessSwiftSamples/curl: Curl a host url
   (**parameters**: payload)
 action /serverless.swift@roboticsind.com_dev/
ServerlessSwiftSamples/wordCount: Count words in a
string
   (**parameters**: payload)
 action /serverless.swift@roboticsind.com_dev/
ServerlessSwiftSamples/greeting: Returns a friendly
greeting
   (**parameters**: name, place)
 action /serverless.swift@roboticsind.com_dev/
ServerlessSwiftSamples/helloWorld: Demonstrates logging
facilities
   (**parameters**: payload)

Notice that all the actions in the /whisk.
system/samples package are available in the
ServerlessSwiftSamples package binding.

3. Invoke an action in the *package* binding:

```
$ ibmcloud fn action invoke --result
ServerlessSwiftSamples/greeting --param name Marek
{
    "payload": "Hello, Marek from San Francisco!"
}
```

As it was expected, the *action* inherits the place *parameter* you set when you created the ServerlessSwiftSamples *package* binding.

4. Invoke an *action* and overwrite the default *parameter* value:

```
$ ibmcloud fn action invoke --result
ServerlessSwiftSamples/greeting --param name Michael
--param place Sacramento
{
    "payload": "Hello, Michael from Sacramento!"
}
```

Setting up the place parameter again in the action invocation overwrites the default value set in the ServerlessSwiftSamples package binding.

Options for Serverless Action

You can call Serverless actions synchronously or asynchronously. The preceding examples were synchronous, and you waited for the result to appear. The CLI *blocked* the action activation until completion, and the result was received since the --result flag was provided. This approach is great when developing and testing your actions, and the actions response time is relatively short as there is a default timeout imposed by the command.

If you want to call your action asynchronously, you need to drop the --result command-line option from the action call. In such a case, the Apache OpenWhisk will create an activation ID for the action call. With the activation ID, you can later retrieve the activation record of the action:

```
$ ibmcloud fn action invoke /whisk.system/samples/greeting
ok: invoked /whisk.system/samples/greeting with id 0ab951750e0d
4f49b951750e0d0f4914
```

To retrieve the results of a non-blocking call to an action, you need to use the activation ID to retrieve the record using the form "ibmcloud fn activation get <id>".

For example,

```
$ ibmcloud fn activation get 0ab951750e0d4f49b951750e0d0f4914
ok: got activation 0ab951750e0d4f49b951750e0d0f4914
{
    "namespace": "serverless.swift@roboticsind.com_dev",
    "name": "greeting",
    "activationId": "0ab951750e0d4f49b951750e0d0f4914",
    "duration": 43,
    "statusCode": 0,
    "response": {
        "status": "success",
        "statusCode": 0,
        "success": true,
        "result": {
            "payload": "Hello, stranger from somewhere!"
        }
    },
    "logs": [
        "2020-04-13T14:48:37.555609Z    stdout: params: {}"
    ],
...
}
```

If you want to explicitly block on a call and see the entire activation and not just the result, you can alternatively use the --blocking parameter on the CLI call:

```
$ ibmcloud fn action invoke /whisk.system/samples/greeting
--blocking
ok: invoked /whisk.system/samples/greeting with id 3a88680e1907
434988680e1907534926
{
    "activationId": "3a88680e1907434988680e1907534926",
    ...
    "response": {
        "result": {
            "payload": "Hello, stranger from somewhere!"
        },
        "size": 45,
        "status": "success",
        "success": true
    },
    ...
}
```

A blocking invocation request will wait for the activation result for the lesser of 60 seconds[3] (this is the default for blocking invocations) or the action's configured time limit. If the result is available during that blocking wait period, it is going to be returned; otherwise, the action continues, and it returns the activation ID as in the non-blocking invocation requests. Shall the action request exceed its invocation time limits, the activation record will indicate this error.

---

[3]Both blocking invocations using either result or blocking flags suffer the same timeout which is set/imposed by the platform provider.

Some of the useful commands[4] for working with activations are as follows:

1. Lists all activations:

```
$ ibmcloud fn activation list
```

2. Shows the last activation:

```
$ ibmcloud fn activation get --last
```

3. Shows only the results of the activation:

```
$ ibmcloud fn activation result <ID>
```

If you decide to go down the rabbit hole to understand the details of the activation record, you might find some important information contained within them. The activation record obviously contains the JSON dictionary values of the result, which shows the value that is returned by the action. In addition, you will find the name and namespace of the entity and the times of start and end in Unix time format. Especially useful in the debugging process, any log output produced by the action during the activation will also be shown. You can check a log output with the TIMESTAMP STREAM and LOG LINEs.

Of special note for debugging, you can also check annotations, that is, key-value pairs recording metadata about the action activation which often contain provider-specific metadata. Metadata include the response status of the activation, that is, "success," and also the information on a failed result such as "application error," the "action developer error," or a "whisk internal error". These status results are also codified using 0–3 numbers. If the activation wasn't successful, the result field would contain the error key with the failure description.

---

[4]Check the Apache OpenWhisk for full set of commands.

Web actions

One of the special ways to make actions easily accessible is by making them into web actions.[5] Web actions are actions that are accessible through a simple REST interface without the need for credentials.[6] However, if there is a need for authentication and authorization or OAuth flow, you can easily enable security on the web action.

Note   When you create a web action, the result is a URL that can be used to trigger the action from any web app.

The other reason to use web actions is to leverage any type of HTTP request. Web actions can be invoked with GET, POST, PUT, PATCH, and DELETE, as well as HEAD and OPTIONS.

Moreover, you are able to trigger a web action from anywhere. When you create an IBM Cloud Functions web action, you generate a URL to invoke that action from any web-based app. Actions that are not web actions require authentication. To get the URL of a web action, you can run the following command: `ibmcloud fn action get <action_name> --url`; check the following example:

```
$ ibmcloud fn action get rule-serverless-swift-cli/helloworld
--url
ok: got action helloworld
https://us-south.functions.cloud.ibm.com/api/v1/namespaces/
serverless.swift%40roboticsind.com_dev/actions/rule-serverless-
swift-cli/helloworld
```

---

[5]https://cloud.ibm.com/docs/openwhisk?topic=cloud-functions-actions_web

[6]A web accessible action is used for, for example, a browser usage to serve up different content type and CORS enablement.

The resulting URL is structured as follows: `https://<apihost>/api/v1/web/<namespace>/<packageName>/<actionName>.<ext>`. This URL (a web action API path) you can use with *cURL* and *wget* or even be entered directly in your browser.[7]

Furthermore, web actions can be used to implement HTTP handlers that respond with headers, statusCode, and body content of different types. Web actions must return a JSON object like in a regular action. However, the controller treats a web action differently if its result includes one or more of the properties as top-level JSON properties.

The important part of calling web action is its HTTP response. The default Content-Type for an HTTP response is `application/json`, and the body can be any allowed JSON value. In other situations than the default `application/json`, you need to define a Content-Type in the headers of your action code.

Note   If the size limit for the result returned by an action is reached, the response fails. If you know that your action result is larger than 5 MB,[8] then you may want to set up a Cloud object store to store the result and return a reference to the result object to be retrieved separately.

Finally, thanks to web actions, you would create fewer Cloud Functions entities. The main reason for that is because you can invoke a web action from anywhere, you are not required to create other Cloud Functions entities like triggers or rules. Cloud Functions actions can be web-enabled by setting the `--web true` flag in the action create command or on a subsequent update command. You can also create a web action from multiple app files by packaging them as a .zip archive. You can also create a web action by using Docker images.

---

[7]Please note that the .ext part may be going away as confusing and of little value.
[8]The size cap might change by the vendor's decision.

Feeds and event providers

Examples of events include changes to database records, IoT sensor readings that exceed a certain temperature, new code commits to a GitHub repository, or simple HTTP requests from web or mobile apps. Events from external and internal event sources and various types of event providers can be channeled through triggers and rules that invoke actions that react to these events using feeds that are packaged as event providers. Feeds are implemented as specialized actions that adhere to an OpenWhisk standard interface. If you look at the feed from the architectural pattern point of view, they typically interact with external event sources in three typical ways: Hooks, Polling, and Connections.

Hooks

The simplest feed pattern reacts to events generated by an existing webhook[9] facility that is exposed by another service. Effectively, the external service's webhook would POST event data directly to the feed's URL in order to fire a trigger. This is a particularly convenient option when designing low-frequency feeds.

Polling

The "Polling" pattern typically works with an integrated alarm service to cause the OpenWhisk feed action to fetch new data from an endpoint by periodically polling it. As it is easy to build, the frequency of discovered events is limited by the polling interval. This pattern is often used when a webhook facility is not available and real-time event processing using actions is not required.

---

[9]A webhook – a user defined HTTP callback – `https://en.wikipedia.org/wiki/Webhook`

Connections

In this pattern, you would stand up a separate service that maintains a persistent "connection" to a feed source. The connected service would be verified via long polling or would be equipped with the push notification mechanism. Hosting a dedicated service is the option that should be used when real-time event processing is needed and a webhook facility is not available.

Difference between feed and trigger

In the next section, you will learn more on triggers, which are closely related to feeds, but different technically.

A trigger might be perceived as a name for a class of events that flow into the system. Each event is associated with the one particular trigger. You can compare a trigger to a topic in a topic-based publish-subscribe system. The rule described as "T->A" should be understood as "when an event from trigger T arrives, invoke the action A with the trigger payload."

A feed on the other hand is a stream of events. These events belong to a trigger T. A feed action controls the feed. The feed action handles creating, deleting, pausing, and resuming the stream of events that comprise a feed. The action feed interacts with external services that are producers of events by REST API calls managing notifications.

Implementing feed actions

For the most part, a feed action is a normal action, but you need to provide support for the following parameters:

- lifecycle event[10] – One of "CREATE", "READ", "UPDATE", "DELETE", "PAUSE", or "UNPAUSE"

- triggerName – The fully qualified name of the trigger which contains events produced from this feed

- authKey – The basic auth credentials of the OpenWhisk user who owns the trigger just mentioned

You might want to add additional parameters to the feed action that your action might need.

When the user creates a trigger from the CLI with the --feed parameter, the system automatically invokes the feed action with these feed parameters with different lifecycle events.

Rules and triggers

As you have learned in the previous sections, the events from external and internal event sources are channeled through a trigger. The rules allow actions to react to these events.

Triggers define a channel for a particular type of event. You might have triggers for location update events, uploads of documents to a website, or incoming emails. You can use a dictionary of key-value pairs to fire a trigger. In some cases, you will refer to such the dictionary as an event. As it was demonstrated before with actions, each firing of a trigger produces an activation ID.

Triggers can be explicitly fired by a user or fired on behalf of a user by an external event source. A feed is a convenient way to configure an external event source to fire trigger events that can be consumed by

---

[10]You should perform certain tasks relative to the event provider the feed is acting as a proxy for. You might find more details at the official Apache OpenWhisk website.

OpenWhisk. Some of such situations will include the Cloudant data change feed that fires a trigger event whenever there is a change of a document (a "CRUD" operation as for Create, Read, Update, Delete) in a database, or a Git feed would fire a trigger event for every commit to a Git repository.

On the other hand, a rule associates one trigger with one action. When a trigger is being fired, OpenWhisk invokes the corresponding action with the trigger event as input. This association is many to many, it is possible that a single trigger event invokes multiple actions, or an action is being invoked in response to events coming from multiple triggers. That is a typical scenario seen in conjunctions with an image classification by an AI service like the classifyImage action that detects the objects in an image and classifies them or the thumbnailImage action that creates a thumbnail version of an image.

The additional perspective gives the example with the situation shown in Figure 5-1.

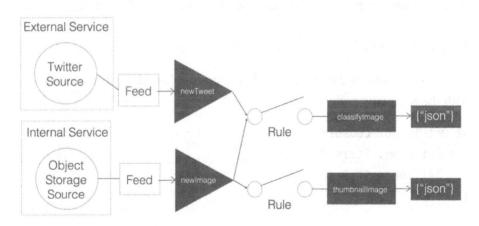

Figure 5-1. *Rules and triggers demonstrated*

As you can see from the picture, two rules[11] allow for images to get visual classifications from a tweet as well as from an uploaded picture, in addition to a thumbnail image being generated for any uploaded image.

Triggers can be fired when certain events occur or can be fired manually. In the next steps, you will create a trigger that is sending the user location updates, and then you will manually fire the trigger.

A trigger that is fired without an accompanying rule to match against has no visible effect. Triggers cannot be created inside a package; they must be created directly under a namespace.

Rules are used to associate a trigger with an action. Each time a trigger event is fired, the action is invoked with the event parameters.

As an example, you can create a rule that calls the `helloworld` action whenever a location update is posted. You can update a "`helloworld.swift`" file with the new action code. You might want to start from the earlier used GitHub repository (you might want to clone it again following these instructions):

```
$ git clone https://github.com/serverless-swift/helloworld-cli.git
$ cd helloworld-cli/
```

Now edit your `helloworld.swift` file and replace the content of the file with the following code:

```
struct Input: Codable {
    let name: String?
    let loc:  String?
}
```

---

[11]The rule is a simple "on/off switch." In fact, it should be noted that IBM Cloud Functions doesn't expose the rule to users in the web interface at all.

```swift
struct Output: Codable {
    let greeting: String
}

    func main(param: Input, completion: (Output?, Error?) ->
    Void) -> Void {
    let result = Output(greeting: "Hello \(param.name ??
    "stranger") from \(param.loc ?? "somewhere")!")
    completion(result, nil)
}
```

Now you can create the new action:

```
PACKAGE_NAME=rule-serverless-swift-cli ibmcloud fn deploy -m
manifest.yaml
```

Now you can test this action:

```
$ ibmcloud fn action invoke --result rule-serverless-swift-cli/
helloworld
```

It should return something like that:

```
{
    "greeting": "Hello stranger from somewhere!"
}
```

You can enter the following command to create the trigger:

```
$ ibmcloud fn trigger create locationUpdate
ok: created trigger locationUpdate
```

Check that you created the trigger by listing the set of triggers:

```
$ ibmcloud fn trigger list
triggers
/serverless.swift@roboticsind.com_dev/
locationUpdate                         private
```

So far you've created a named "channel" to which events can be fired. Now let's make sure that the trigger and action exist:

```
$ ibmcloud fn trigger update locationUpdate
ok: updated trigger locationUpdate
```

```
$ ibmcloud fn action update rule-serverless-swift-cli/
helloworld actions/helloworld.swift
ok: updated action rule-serverless-swift-cli/helloworld
```

Now you are ready to create the rule. The three parameters are the name of the rule, the trigger, and the action.

Note   The rule will be enabled upon creation, meaning that it will be immediately available to respond to activations of your trigger.

```
$ ibmcloud fn rule create myRule locationUpdate rule-
serverless-swift-cli/helloworld
ok: created rule myRule
```

Next, fire a trigger event by specifying the trigger name and parameters. Each time that you fire an event, the hello action is called with the event parameters:

```
$ ibmcloud fn trigger fire locationUpdate --param name Marek
--param loc "San Francisco"
ok: triggered /_/locationUpdate with id
a84a609f4f3445e98a609f4f34e5e9d0
```

Verify that the action was invoked by checking the most recent activation:

```
$ ibmcloud fn  activation list --limit 1 rule-serverless-swift-
cli/helloworld
```

You should see something like:

```
Datetime               Activation
ID                     Kind    Start Duration   Status  Entity
2020-04-25 20:41:46 432e183852e042e0ae183852e082e004 swift:4.2
warm  2ms              success serverless...com_dev/helloworld:0.0.4
```

You see that the hello action received the event payload and returned the expected string using the activation ID:

```
$ ibmcloud fn activation result
432e183852e042e0ae183852e082e004
{
    "greeting": "Hello Marek from San Francisco!"
}
```

You can create multiple rules that associate the same trigger with different actions. Triggers and rules cannot belong to a package. The rule may be associated with an action that belongs to a package however, for example:

```
$ ibmcloud fn rule create recordLocation locationUpdate /whisk.
system/utils/echo
ok: created rule recordLocation
```

You can also use rules with sequences.[12] For example, one can create an action sequence recordLocationAndHello that is activated by the rule anotherRule:

```
$ ibmcloud fn action create recordLocationAndHello --sequence /
whisk.system/utils/echo,rule-serverless-swift-cli/helloworld
ok: created action recordLocationAndHello
```

---

[12]You will find more information on sequences at the end of this chapter.

```
$ ibmcloud fn rule create anotherRule locationUpdate
recordLocationAndHello
ok: created rule anotherRule
```

List all the rules:

```
$ ibmcloud fn rule list
rules
/serverless.swift@roboticsind.com_dev/
anotherRule                        private              active
/serverless.swift@roboticsind.com_dev/
recordLocation                     private              active
/serverless.swift@roboticsind.com_dev/myRu
le                           private              active
```

And in any time, you can disable the rule:

```
$ ibmcloud fn rule disable myRule
ok: disabled rule myRule
```

iOS SDK

OpenWhisk provides a mobile SDK for iOS and watchOS devices that enables mobile apps to fire remote triggers and invoke remote actions. A version for Android is not available. Android developers can use the OpenWhisk REST API directly. The mobile SDK is written in Swift 4.x and supports iOS 11 and later releases. You can build the mobile SDK by using Xcode 9 or later.

Note   At the time of writing this book, the mobile SDK is not supported for IAM-based namespaces. Use a Cloud Foundry-based namespace instead.

You can install the mobile SDK by using popular package managers for Apple iOS and Apple WatchOS apps: CocoaPods and Carthage, or alternatively you can choose to build the SDK from the source directory of Apache OpenWhisk GitHub project.[13] In addition to that, IBM Cloud Functions provides you with a sample application that you have learned to use in Chapter 4.

In order to connect to OpenWhisk, use WhiskCredentials object with your OpenWhisk API credentials and create an OpenWhisk instance from the object. For example, use the following example code to create a credentials object:

```
let credentialsConfiguration = WhiskCredentials(accessKey:
"myKey", accessToken: "myToken")
let whisk = Whisk(credentials: credentialsConfiguration!)
```

In the previous example, you pass in the myKey and myToken that you get from OpenWhisk. You can retrieve the key and token with the following CLI command:

```
$ ibmcloud fn property get --auth
whisk auth              kkkkkkkk:ttttttttttttttttttttttttttt
```

The string before the colon is your key, and the string after the colon is your token.

With the OpenWhisk credentials set, you are ready to invoke a remote action. You can call invokeAction with the action name. Use a dictionary to pass parameters to the action as needed.

In the same way, you can fire a remote trigger. Simply you can call the fireTrigger method and pass in parameters as needed by using a dictionary:

---

[13]Find some further documentation on that in IBM Cloud Docs: https://cloud.ibm.com/docs/openwhisk?topic=cloud-functions-pkg_mobile_sdk

```
// In this example we are firing a trigger when our location
has changed by a certain amount
var locationParams = Dictionary<String, String>()
locationParams["payload"] = "{\"lat\":37.788157, \"lon\":-
122.396228}" //San Francisco, IBM Watson West
do {
    try whisk.fireTrigger(name: "locationChanged", package:
    "rule-serverless-swift-cli", namespace: "serverless.swift@
    roboticsind.com_dev", parameters: locationParams, callback:
    {(reply, error) -> Void in
        if let error = error {
            print("Error firing trigger \(error.
            localizedDescription)")
        } else {
            print("Trigger fired!")
        }
    })
} catch {
    print("Error \(error)")
}
```

If the action returns a result, set hasResult to true in the invokeAction call. The result of the action is returned in the reply dictionary, for example:

```
do {
    try whisk.invokeAction(name: "actionWithResult", package:
"rule-serverless-swift-cli", namespace: "serverless.swift@
roboticsind.com_dev", parameters: params, hasResult: true,
callback: {(reply, error) -> Void in
        if let error = error {
            //do something
```

```
            print("Error invoking Action \(error.
            localizedDescription)")
        } else {
            var result = reply["result"]
            print("Got result \(result)")
        }
    })
} catch {
    print("Error \(error)")
}
```

Note   By default, the SDK returns only the `activation` ID and
any result that is produced by the invoked action. To get metadata of
the entire response object, which includes the HTTP response status
code, use the following setting: `whisk.verboseReplies` = `true`.

You can configure the SDK to work with different installations of
OpenWhisk by using the baseURL parameter. If you use an installation
that is running at `http://localhost:8080`, you can specify the following
baseURL:

```
whisk.baseURL = "http://localhost:8080"
```

You can pass in a custom `NSURLSession` in case you require special
network handling. For example, you might have your own OpenWhisk
installation that uses self-signed certificates.

All actions and triggers have a fully qualified name that is made up of
a namespace, a package, and an action or trigger name. As you have seen,
the SDK accepts these elements as parameters when you are invoking
an action or firing a trigger. You can also provide a fully qualified name
to a function in the SDK that looks like /mynamespace/mypackage/

nameOfActionOrTrigger. The qualified name string supports unnamed default values for namespaces and packages that all OpenWhisk users have, so the following parsing rules apply:

```
qName = "foo" results in namespace = default, package =
default, action/trigger = "foo"
qName = "mypackage/foo" results in namespace = default, package
= mypackage, action/trigger = "foo"
qName = "/mynamespace/foo" results in namespace = mynamespace,
package = default, action/trigger = "foo"
qName = "/mynamespace/mypackage/foo" results in namespace =
mynamespace, package = mypackage, action/trigger = "foo"
```

All other combinations issue a WhiskError.QualifiedName error. Therefore, when you are using qualified names, you must wrap the call in a "do/try/catch" construct.

Finally, for convenience of iOS developers, the SDK includes a WhiskButton, which extends the UIButton to allow it to invoke actions.

Entities, namespaces, and permissions

You might want to better understand how IBM Cloud Functions enforces access control on entities using namespaces. Namespaces logically contain other Cloud Functions entities, such as actions and triggers, and belong to a resource group. You can let users access your Cloud Functions entities by granting them access to the namespace. This allows for a very basic set of permissions to your Serverless backend.

> **Note**   With the Cloud Functions CLI plug-in, you don't need to explicitly configure the API key and API host. Instead, you can log in with `ibmcloud login`. You can target an IAM-enabled namespace by running `ibmcloud fn property set --namespace <namespace_name>` or a Cloud Foundry-based namespace by running `ibmcloud target --cf`. After you log in, all commands begin with `ibmcloud fn`.

Cloud Functions actions, triggers, and rules belong in a namespace and sometimes packages which, as we learned, can contain actions and feeds. However, we also noted that entities do not have to be contained in a package.

You can create new IAM-based namespaces by running `ibmcloud fn namespace create`. *Cloud Foundry*-based namespaces are made from a combination of an `org` and a `space` name. For example, if you are targeted to the `serverless.swift@roboticsinventions.com` org and the dev space, then you are targeting the Cloud Functions *Cloud Foundry*-based namespace called `serverless.swift@roboticsinventions.com_dev`.

> **Limitations**   The `/whisk.system` namespace is reserved for entities that are distributed with the Cloud Functions system. Mind that the *Serverless Framework* or iOS SDK doesn't support IAM-based namespaces. However, IBM Cloud is moving away from CF namespaces and IAM namespaces are now the default. Also, some event provider services may still require CF namespaces, and you may need to create them manually within IBM Cloud via an interface that is not part of the IBM Cloud Functions web UI.

If you need to use the authentication API key for Cloud Functions in an external HTTP client such as *cURL* or *Postman*, you can retrieve it with the following command:

```
$ ibmcloud iam oauth-tokens
```

In addition, in order to get the current Cloud Foundry API key, you need to run the following command:

```
$ ibmcloud fn property get --auth
```

It is relatively easy to get the current API host; simply type the following command:

```
$ ibmcloud fn property get --apihost
```

Note   The API key is specific per region, organization, and space targeted by the Cloud Functions CLI plug-in.

Changing the name of the org or space creates a new namespace based on the changed name. The entities in the old namespace are not visible in the new namespace and might be deleted.

Since IBM Cloud Functions is enabled for identity and access management (IAM), you can use IAM across IBM Cloud to control access to resources by users or applications. IAM simplifies access control over your functions' resources and other IBM Cloud resources, like service instances. IAM allows for creating managed namespaces in order to group entities, namely, actions or triggers, and define IAM access policies for the newly created namespace. In addition to Policies, IAM also uses Identities and Resources to control access.

In the IAM context, Policies define certain access rules. You can refer to Policies as to Roles, since they define an access role for certain Identities on certain Resources. Your Policy could, for example, define that the

Identity – a user – has a *read* access to a Resource that might be a Cloud Functions namespace. In addition to the namespace, the Resources in the IBM Cloud also represent instances of services, like provisioned database instances, or container clusters. Identities are the *subjects* that require access to IBM Cloud resources. Usually, an identity is represented by a user or a user group. IAM also supports Service Identities, which represent a functional user for an application or a service.

When defining a new Cloud Functions namespace, also a new Service Identity is being created. This Service Identity is like a functional user representing the new namespace. You will use this Identity to manage the access of namespace actions to other resources and services. In addition to the Service Identity, the API key is going to be associated with it. You can use this API key as a token to access an IAM-enabled IBM Cloud resource.

There are two different access flows for Cloud Functions: the *inbound* and the *outbound* flows.

When you access or invoke a Cloud Function, this is the *inbound* flow. In order to access a function, you need to provide an IAM token to the IAM-enabled namespace. This token is checked against the access control defined for the associated identity within a namespace and given roles (a *Writer* access role can modify the action, and a *Reader* access can only read the action code or invoke the action).

The *outbound* access is the case when your action code calls out to another IBM Cloud service or resource. If that is an IAM-enabled resource, the action code must provide a token for authentication. For this purpose, IBM Cloud is creating one service identity for each namespace which can be used as a functional ID to access IBM Cloud resources.

Sequences

OpenWhisk allows you to compose actions together in a *sequence*, which makes it a powerful programming tool. A *sequence* is a chain of actions, invoked in order, where the output of one becomes the input to the next.

Sequences allow you to combine existing actions together for quick and easy reuse. You can invoke a *sequence* just like an action, through a REST API or via an automated process in a rule. Sequences can use standard actions as well as web actions.

In order to create a sequence from the console, you can use actions that are available in your namespace or any public actions; you need to select a namespace that is going to contain your IBM Cloud Functions entities. The process is intuitive and starts from the Cloud Functions console (Figure 5-2).

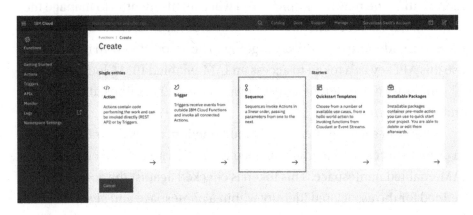

Figure 5-2. *Creating a sequence from the console*

You need to specify a sequence name, its package, and the initial action for your sequence. You can choose existing actions, available in your namespace, or else select a public action. When you are ready, finish by clicking the Create button, and then add one or more actions to your sequence and Save (Figure 5-3). You can test your code by clicking Invoke (Figure 5-4).

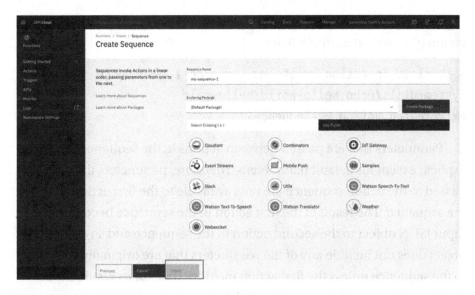

Figure 5-3. *Adding existing or public actions to a sequence from the console*

Figure 5-4. *Invoking a sequence from the console*

A very similar process is in the CLI with the ibmcloud fn action create command – see an example here:

```
$ ibmcloud fn action create my-sequence-2 --sequence /whisk.
system/utils/echo,hello-world/helloworld
ok: created action my-sequence-2
```

Parameters that are passed between actions in the sequence are explicit, except for default parameters. Therefore, parameters that are passed to the action sequence are only available to the first action in the sequence. The result of the first action in the sequence becomes the input JSON object to the second action in the sequence and so on. This object does not include any of the parameters that are originally passed to the sequence unless the first action includes them in its result. Input parameters to an action are merged with the action's default parameters, with the former taking precedence and overriding any matching default parameters.

A sequence does not have limits that are separate from those limits of each action that is contained within the sequence. While you can set limits for timeout, memory, and logsize when you create a sequence, those limits are ignored. Note that the limits configured for each action in the sequence are individually enforced. Mind the fact that a sequence is a pipeline of actions. Therefore, a failure in one action breaks the entire pipeline.

After you create a sequence, it is effectively treated as an action itself by OpenWhisk. You can use its name when you create a rule or invoke it as a normal action with parameters and apply other action features to it such as making it a web action.

Summary

This concludes our Apache OpenWhisk deep dive. Having immersed yourself in all this Serverless information, you are ready to create robust Serverless applications, taking full advantage of IBM Cloud Functions! Let's get started with programming some using Serverless Swift in iOS applications with an open source code example.

CHAPTER 6

The Complete iOS App Using Serverless Swift

In this chapter, you will be introduced to typical development strategies using Serverless Swift in an iOS app. You will build a basic AI powered app[1] and then leverage the Serverless backend for Cloud-based functionality. The Serverless actions will be responsible for analyzing the Hacker News articles with the AI service – Watson Natural Language Understanding (NLU) in order to detect keywords, entities, and categories in the article.

The mobile app reads articles from Hacker News and analyzes them with NLU for keywords, entities, and so on. If there is no analysis available, it requests Watson AI service to read it.

Step 1. The architecture overview

You can start the process of building an app with its Serverless Mobile Backend-as-a-Service (Serverless MBaaS for short). Refer to Figure 6-1 to understand what elements are involved (an app on a phone, actions in the Cloud, APIs at some other Cloud).

---

[1]The full app is made available in the Apress GitHub repository for this book – check it out here: `https://github.com/serverless-swift/ch6-app`

© Marek Sadowski and Lennart Frantzell 2020
M. Sadowski and L. Frantzell, *Serverless Swift*,
https://doi.org/10.1007/978-1-4842-5836-1_6

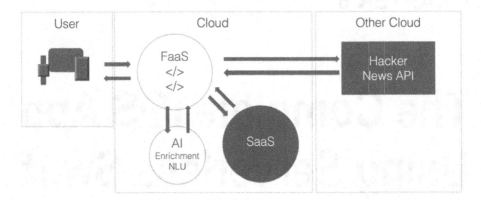

Figure 6-1. *The app with Serverless MBaaS architecture chart overview*

This application is going to list the Hacker News items from the Y Combinator Portal and analyze those displayed. In this example, you would see the efficiency of the parallel Action calls.

We will use three use cases, namely, the Serverless backend, the Mobile Serverless Backend, and the AI data processing use case that we will describe in more detail in Chapter 7.

Note   You are going to use the Minimal Viable Product approach. That means in the first prototype, you will develop a basic reader app enriched with the data from Watson AI service: Natural Language Understanding. You may then take it further to produce more advanced prototypes, as the content of the app is provided as an Open Source with the Apache 2 license.

Step 2. Setup of the mobile app

Let's start by cloning a scaffold of our mobile app. Our mobile app is using the table view for presenting particular articles, as well as keywords, entities, and classifications from the NLU analysis.

We'll start by cloning the existing application that was made available for you through the code repository at github.com for this chapter – you can either download the code as a zip file from `https://github.com/serverless-swift/ch6-app` or you might want to use a git command if it is available on your operating system:

```
$ git clone https://github.com/serverless-swift/ch6-app
```

And the rest of commands for the repository remain the same:

```
$ cd ch6-app/01-basic-app
```

Now you can use CocoaPods and the command `pod install` to get the required components for the application:

```
$ pod install
```

As soon as this command finishes, you are able to open the `hacker-news.xcworkspace` project (it is important to open `.xcworkspace` since it has all the downloaded dependencies).

Now you can test the app to see the UI by simply starting the app and using the play button of the application – see Figure 6-2.

Figure 6-2. *Starting the hacker-news app in the simulator in the Xcode IDE*

Feel free to change the simulated device, or if you have an Apple Developer License, use your phone to test the static app. As soon as your static mobile app runs, you should see something like the screenshot from Figure 6-3 on your simulator.

Figure 6-3. *Simulating the static app for Hacker News reader*

Step 3. Provisioning of free services in the IBM Cloud

You will be provisioning the DB Cloudant and Watson Natural Language Understanding (NLU for short) services. See Figure 6-4 for selecting the NLU service by using the search function.

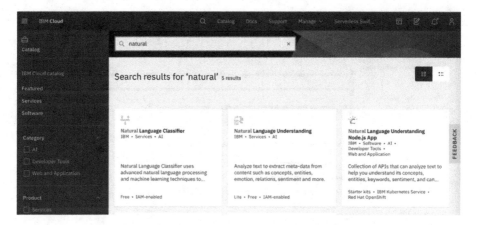

Figure 6-4. *Adding IBM Watson Natural Language Understanding service*

If you haven't done so before, you need to sign up to IBM Cloud in order to provision the services (see Appendix 1 for the details).

After these services are provisioned for your selected region, you might want to use the US South (Dallas) data center like shown here. And now you are ready to create the first actions.

Step 4. The flow chart of the Serverless backend

The second part of the system is the Serverless backend. Let's have a look into the detailed diagram showing interactions among a mobile app, serverless actions, their sequences, Cloud-based SaaS services, and the Hacker News APIs. Check Figure 6-5.

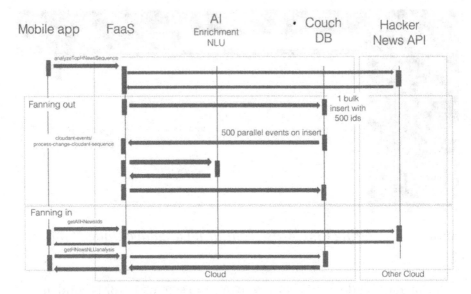

Figure 6-5. *Serverless Mobile Backend consisting of sequences and actions*

Step 5. The core NLU action

You might want to refer to the official documents describing the use of Serverless Swift with Apache OpenWhisk.[2] Let's start with adding the precompiled Docker-based Swift actions. There are two reasons for you needing to use multiple file Docker-based actions:

- To include additional libraries and repositories that are needed for our deployments – you would need access to the networking like KituraNet project, CloudantSwift project, or SwiftyJSON project and the respective WatsonDeveloperCloud SDK including Natural Language Understanding SDK.

---

[2]https://github.com/ibm-functions/runtime-swift

- In order to pre-warm the cold start of actions – more on this in Chapter 8 – when using Docker and precompiled actions.

In order to start the process, let's prepare a basic setup based on the multiple file recipe from the Apache OpenWhisk runtime Swift repository:[3]

- Build the multiple file action folder structure.

- Zip the files.

- Compile them using Docker.

- Update your actions in Apache OpenWhisk environment.

The file structure looks exactly like this:

- Your action folder

  - Package.swift (all the additional dependencies)

  - Source folder (your action Swift source files)

  - Your action(s)

Note   The basic structure and all of the Action code have been provided for you with an exception for the generated code in Step 10 in this chapter by the template generator in IBM Cloud Functions for the Cloudant-based triggers.

---

[3]https://github.com/apache/openwhisk-runtime-swift#packaging-an-action-as-a-swift-executable-using-swift-4x

Step 6. Building a multi-file action in Swift with Docker

Let's start with creating the action to analyze with NLU by providing the URL passed in the parameters. Your action will be called NLUaction, and you are going to call the file NLUanalyze.swift.

You can start by simply using the repository from the previous GitHub clone in Step 2; you need to change the directory to the 02-swift-actions and select the first NLUaction:

```
$ cd 02-swift-actions/NLUaction/
```

Examine the Package.swift:

```
// swift-tools-version:4.2
import PackageDescription

let package = Package(
    name: "Action",
    products: [
    .executable(
        name: "Action",
        targets:  ["Action"]
    )
    ],
dependencies:[.package(url:"https://github.com/watson-
developer-cloud/swift-sdk", from: "3.4.0")
    ],
    targets: [
    .target(
name:"Action",dependencies:["SwiftyRequest",
"NaturalLanguageUnderstandingV1"],
```

```
    path: "."
  )
  ]
)
```

Note   The first line of Package.swift, `//swift-tools-version:4.2`, defines the Swift version being used. It is important to note that the IBM Cloud Functions platform at the time of writing the book is using Swift 4.2 version.

Inspect the Source/nluAnalyze.swift – it is just a simple action that calls to Watson NLU. We are using the semaphore to wait for the result of the analysis:

```
[...some imports and the default code]

let _whisk_semaphore = DispatchSemaphore(value: 0)
// MARK: setting up the apiKey and iamURL in parameters
let authenticator = WatsonIAMAuthenticator(apiKey: "your
APIkey")
let naturalLanguageUnderstanding = NaturalLanguageUnderstanding
(version: "2019-07-12", authenticator: authenticator)
  naturalLanguageUnderstanding.serviceURL = "https://api.us-
  south.natural-language-understanding.watson.cloud.ibm.com/
  instances/<your instance here>"

  let keywords = KeywordsOptions(limit: 5)
  let concepts = ConceptsOptions(limit: 2)
  let entities = EntitiesOptions(limit: 2)
  let categories = CategoriesOptions(limit: 3)
```

```swift
    let features = Features(concepts: concepts, emotion:
    EmotionOptions(), entities: entities, keywords:
    keywords, sentiment: SentimentOptions(), categories:
    CategoriesOptions())

    naturalLanguageUnderstanding.analyze(features: features,
url: param.newsUrl ?? "https://openwhisk.apache.org/") {
        response, error in

        guard let analysis = response?.result else {
            print(error?.localizedDescription ?? "unknown error")
                _whisk_semaphore.signal()
            return
        }
[... Some detailed analysis here ...]

        result = Output(keywords: analysis.keywords?.description
        as! String, entities: analysis.entities?.description as!
        String, concepts: analysis.concepts?.description as! String,
        categories: analysis.categories?.description as! String)
        _whisk_semaphore.signal()
    }
    _ = _whisk_semaphore.wait(timeout: .distantFuture)
    completion(result, nil)
}
```

Step 7. Deploying of multi-file action in IBM Cloud

As it is defined in Step 5, when you are ready with the 02-swift-actions/ NLUaction files, use the following zip command:

```
$ zip ../action-src.zip -r *
```

Then run this command to compile your source code:

```
$ docker run -i openwhisk/action-swift-v4.2 -compile main <../
action-src.zip >../action-bin.zip
```

Alternatively, you might want to run just one liner using a Unix pipe "|" instead of two previous commands, if you are familiar with the preceding process:

```
$ zip - -r * | docker run -i openwhisk/action-swift-v4.2
-compile main >../action.zip
```

Now you need to add/update the action (do not forget to log in to IBM Cloud and connect to IBM Cloud Functions backend first – check the steps in Chapter 4, section "Create a Hello World from a command-line interface" – refer to Step 1 and following). Here goes the recap of logging in:

```
$ ibmcloud login -a cloud.ibm.com -o "<your organization>" -s
"<your sub-group>"
$ ibmcloud target -g Default
$ ibmcloud fn list
Entities in namespace: default
packages
```

...

Also the good practice is to use the packages, getting all the required actions together for the project. In your case, the package might be "hacker-news-pak". Let's create such a package and add all next actions to it, instead of adding your actions to the default package:

```
$ ibmcloud fn package create hacker-news-pak
ok: created package hacker-news-pak
```

Let's list all packages:

```
$ ibmcloud fn package list
packages
/serverless.swift@roboticsind.com_dev/hacker-news-
pak                          private
/serverless.swift@roboticsind.com_dev/hello-world-serverless-
swift-cli private
/serverless.swift@roboticsind.com_dev/hello-
world                          private
```

And as soon as everything compiles, you are ready to deploy your action. The "action update" command works as well as "action create" if used on the given action for the first time:

```
$ ibmcloud fn action update hacker-news-pak/NLUaction ../
action.zip --kind swift:4.2
ok: updated action hacker-news-pak/NLUaction
```

And you can test it to see if it works:

```
$ ibmcloud fn action invoke hacker-news-pak/NLUaction --blocking
invoked /_/hacker-news-pak/NLUaction with id
f15830eb7fe14fb09830eb7fe18fb0d9
{
    "activationId": "f15830eb7fe14fb09830eb7fe18fb0d9",

[....]
}
```

Step 8. Fanning out the initial action

Let's start with the Serverless Mobile Backend calls. First, you need to prepare an action to start the process, so obtain all the Hacker News Ids. This action would obtain a result like shown in Figure 6-6.

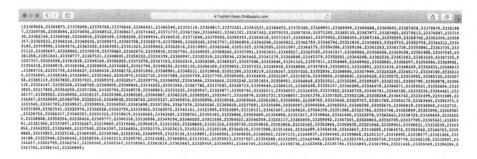

Figure 6-6. *All the Hacker News Ids*

Pattern – fanning out (used to make the process parallel)

The next step is to initiate the process of analyzing with AI the articles for all the top 500 Hacker News; the best would be to do it to only new articles and in parallel. Therefore, we can use the described process in the patterns called fanning out, meaning we would divide the tasks among various processes which could call NLU in separate threads. The results you would present to a user as soon as they become available.

The first action is to read top 500 news – first action getAllHNewsIds will retrieve 500 top news using the provided Hacker News API – check the README.md for the details:

```
$ cd 02-swift-actions/GetAllHNewsIds
$ zip - -r * | docker run -i openwhisk/action-swift-v4.2
-compile main >../action.zip

$ ibmcloud fn action update hacker-news-pak/getAllHNewsIds ../
action.zip --kind swift:4.2
ok: updated action hacker-news-pak/getAllHNewsIds

$ ibmcloud fn action invoke hacker-news-pak/getAllHNewsIds
--blocking
ok: invoked /_/hacker-news-pak/getAllHNewsIds with id
df9ceebab482468a9ceebab482868aec
{
```

```
    "activationId": "df9ceebab482468a9ceebab482868aec",
    "annotations": [
        {
            "key": "path",
            "value": "serverless.swift@roboticsind.com_dev/
            hacker-news-pak/getAllHNewsIds"
        },

        [... some key value pairs..],
    "duration": 3374,
    "end": 1590941364013,
    "logs": [],
    "name": "getAllHNewsIds",
    "namespace": "serverless.swift@roboticsind.com_dev",
    "publish": false,
    "response": {
        "result": {
            "newsIds": [
                23369604,
                23369873,
                23370009,
                23369488,
                23366546,
                23369817,
                23368453,
                23369999,
[top 500 Hacker News Ids]
                23355140,
                23357725,
                23340312
            ]
        },
```

```
    "size": 4514,
    "status": "success",
    "success": true
},
"start": 1590941360639,
"subject": "serverless.swift@roboticsind.com",
"version": "0.0.1"
}
```

Step 8. Storing Hacker News IDs in the Cloudant DB

Now you need to create the db for Hacker News IDs – let's call the new database "hacker-news-ids". Using the Cloudant interface, it is fairly easy to create a database. See Figure 6-7.

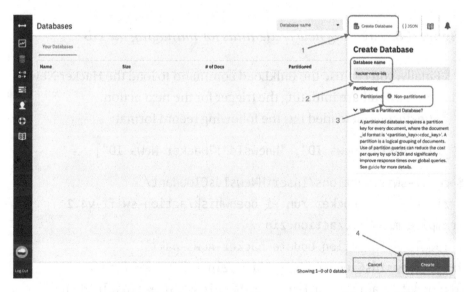

Figure 6-7. *Creating a new DB from the IBM Cloud-based Cloudant DB UI*

Also you will need to create the new credentials to connect to Cloudant from your Serverless Actions. Use the IBM Cloud Cloudant service UI to create those. See Figure 6-8 on how to do it.

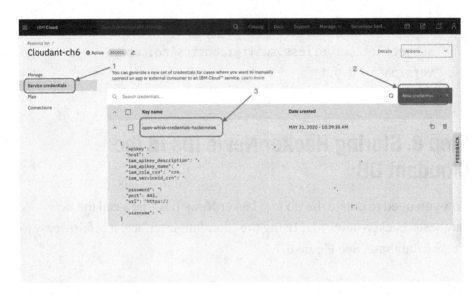

Figure 6-8. *Creating new credentials for managing the DB*

Finally, you can use the BulkLoad command to load the Hacker News Ids into the database initiating the trigger for the next action.

The document loaded has the following record format:

```
["_id":"Hacker News ID", "hnewsId":"Hacker News ID"]

$ cd 02-swift-actions/InsertHNewsIdsCloudant/
$ zip - -r * | docker run -i openwhisk/action-swift-v4.2
-compile main >../action.zip
$ ibmcloud fn action update hacker-news-pak/
insertHNewsIdsCloudant ../action.zip --kind swift:4.2
ok: updated action hacker-news-pak/insertHNewsIdsCloudant
$ ibmcloud fn action invoke hacker-news-pak/
insertHNewsIdsCloudant --blocking
```

```
ok: invoked /_/hacker-news-pak/insertHNewsIdsCloudant,
but the request has not yet finished, with id
82ee97542a8445faae97542a84a5fafd
```

Step 9. Creating the sequence

In order to fetch the data from the external API and make the initial inserts into the Cloudant DB, you need to create and call the sequence from previously created Serverless Actions. Use the following command to create the sequence:[4]

```
$ ibmcloud fn action create hacker-news-pak/
analyzeTopHNewsSequence --sequence hacker-news-pak/
getAllHNewsIds,hacker-news-pak/insertHNewsIdsCloudant
ok: created action hacker-news-pak/analyzeTopHNewsSequence
```

Now with just one call to the hacker-news-pak/ analyzeTopHNewsSequence, your mobile app will start the parallel processing of your request in the Serverless MBaaS.

Step 10. Using the quick template to create a Cloudant DB event listener – triggering an event on insert of a record in Cloudant DB

The package "cloudant-events" generated with the Cloudant template helps you out with triggering all the CREATES in the DB.

Now you can simply update the generated Swift action and include another version with a call to Hacker News API to retrieve all the information available there. See Figure 6-9 for the details.

---

[4]"Mind that gap" – there is no space between actions and the comma like in this example: ibmcloud fn action creates name --sequence a,b,c.

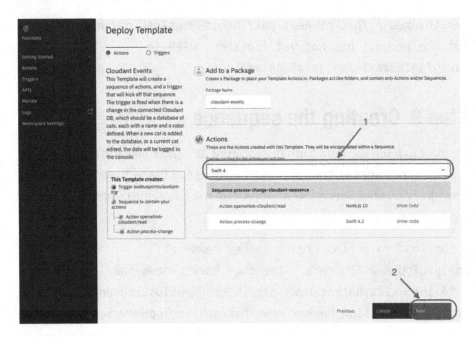

Figure 6-9. *Creating the DB insert event listener with the Templates*

Now, as soon as you get the information back from Hacker News API, you can call the next action with providing the URL the given Hacker News to our previously created NLUaction. See the README.md in the GitHub repository[5] for more information on that.

The goal here is to get the Cloud to start picking the parallel load, through the divide and rule approach. Therefore, you inserted the ids of the articles in the NoSQL database – Cloudant DB – without doubling records, and this should start the process for fanning out of the processing workload.

The second sequence of serverless actions is triggered by Cloudant DB new inserts. The action would look for and fetch the entire news article details from Hacker News API by the provided Hacker News ID. Then the

---

[5]https://github.com/serverless-swift/ch6-app/tree/master/02-swift-actions#creating-the-cloudant-feed-action-from-the-template

next action in the sequence would retrieve the Hacker News URL and pass it over in a sequence to a third action in order to call the Watson NLU service to get the AI analytics of the article. See Figure 6-10 for the details on the content of the Hacker News article by the provided ID.

Figure 6-10. *Details of the Hacker News article*

Step 11. Analyzing the news with Watson NLU service

The third action will analyze with Natural Language Understanding service the article body and provide the results to be referenced to the original record with the Hacker News Id. For that, you would use the following action. Enriching data with AI data processing is a typical use case that is implemented here (more on use cases in Chapter 7).

Note   As a good practice, the action will write to the separate DB in order to avoid any misfire from the event listener.

You can imagine that in parallel all the inserted documents would spring the actions and check a large bulk (up to 500 of those in the initial call!) of documents in the Cloud. This is a beauty of the fanning out and Serverless ramping up without worrying about the resource, management, and operation side.

The sequence looks like this:

  i.   The triggered action with hacker news Id

  ii.   Checking the URL, the title, the Hacker News
        position on the top 500 list

    iii.   Using NLU with the obtained URL

    iv.   Inserting the analysis into the Cloudant DB
(fanning in)

Step 12. Extending the sequence from the template with NLU and inserting results into DB actions

Using the IBM Cloud Functions interface of the sequence created by the template, you can add the next actions in the sequence.

The process to extend the existing sequence made from a template, and adding the next action in the sequence is pretty simple. See Figure 6-11.

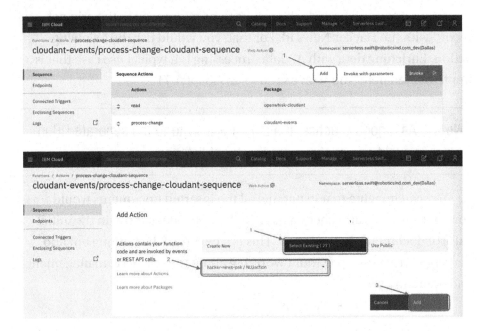

Figure 6-11. *Extending the sequence with NLUaction*

Now you can extend the process even further by adding NLUanalysis2dbAction. You can again use the UI to add the action to the sequence. Instead of a single action, you can imagine invoking analysis sequence. In such a sequence, you will invoke action_a (NLUaction) with the input parameters (the URL and the Hacker News ID for reference). Then action_b (NLUanalysis2dbAction – that would insert the results of the analysis (keywords, entities, and concepts) in the record in the hacker-news-nlu DB in Cloudant) will be invoked with the result from action_a. The result returned by action_b will be returned as the sequence result.

Your total sequence consists of the actions shown in Figure 6-12.

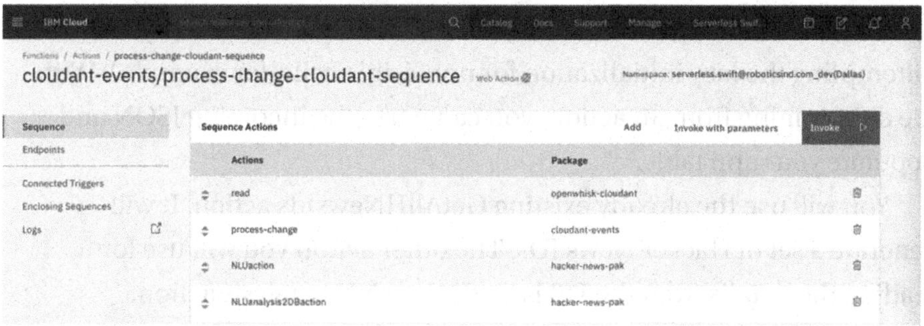

Figure 6-12. *The full action from a triggered read action, through calling NLU action, and finally with storing the action in the dedicated DB*

Shall you want to observe how the actions are being executed, you can use the activation list command and select the specified activation by their IDs to see the details of the call, for example:

```
$ ibmcloud fn activation list
$ ibmcloud fn activation get <provide your activation id here>
```

Step 13. Getting your Hacker News with NLU analysis

The fanning in pattern allows you to consume the results of the "divide and rule" action sequence, following the fanning out pattern from previous steps. The simplest way to get the results now is to create a Serverless function that would read selected records for just the top 10–30 records from Hacker News API (and you have created this action already – it is the getAllHNewsIds action).

Then the app can fill the blanks of the table just by calling the next action that would read the NLU analysis we started in the initial sequence in one of the first steps. The action will call to fill out each empty row (attempting the lazy initialization for nonvisible cells, for example). With the data coming from an action, you can parse the incoming JSON and populate your app table.

You will use the already existing GetAllHNewsIds action. It will generate a set of Hacker News IDs. The other action you will use for reading the details from the DB is GetHNewsNLUanalysis action.

Check the implementation in the respective folders. And compile the actions with provided instructions in the README.md.

Verify if you have all the actions and the sequence:

```
$ ibmcloud fn package get --summary hacker-news-pak
```

You should see the following output:

```
package /serverless.swift@roboticsind.com_dev/hacker-news-pak
   (parameters: none defined)
 action /serverless.swift@roboticsind.com_dev/hacker-news-pak/
 GetHNewsNLUanalysis
   (parameters: none defined)
 action /serverless.swift@roboticsind.com_dev/hacker-news-pak/
 NLUanalysis2DBaction
   (parameters: none defined)
```

```
action /serverless.swift@roboticsind.com_dev/hacker-news-pak/
analyzeTopHNewsSequence
  (parameters: none defined)
action /serverless.swift@roboticsind.com_dev/hacker-news-pak/
insertHNewsIdsCloudant
  (parameters: none defined)
action /serverless.swift@roboticsind.com_dev/hacker-news-pak/
getAllHNewsIds
  (parameters: none defined)
action /serverless.swift@roboticsind.com_dev/hacker-news-pak/
NLUaction
  (parameters: none defined)
```

That means you have a Serverless Mobile Backend-as-a-Service ready. You are ready now to finalize the mobile app and see the analysis of Hacker News with Watson Natural Language Understanding service.

Step 14. Updating the basic app to show the results obtained with help of the Serverless Mobile Backend

After completing the Serverless Mobile Backend, you are finally ready to update the mobile app with the data coming from Hacker News API and results of Watson Natural Language Understanding analysis on the selected top news.

Check the provided folder 03-nlu-app from the cloned GitHub repository, and use CocoaPods instruction pod install from the hacker-news root directory:

```
$ cd 03-nlu-app/hacker-news
$ pod install
```

Now you can open the hacker-news.xcworkspace and analyze the file where we added the calls to the backend. As you might remember from the Hello World application you wrote using the SDK, there are a couple authentication parameters you need to copy from the IBM Cloud Functions. Please refer to Chapter 4 in iOS SDK section on how to update WhiskAppKey and WhiskAppSecret in the NewsTableViewController.swift file in the beginning of the class NewsTableViewController definition. Also update other parameters like your space name (mySpaceName) and your package, and verify names of your actions and sequences. See the screenshot in Figure 6-13.

Figure 6-13. *Defining the keys, secrets, and parameters of the Serverless Mobile Backend-as-a-Service in your mobile iOS app*

As soon as you fill out the required blanks – see the README.md file for that – you are ready to launch the application. See Figure 6-14 for the screenshot of the working app's UI in version 1.0.

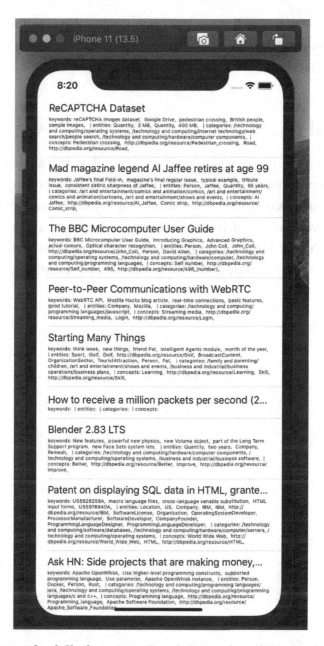

Figure 6-14. *The fully functional mobile reader of Hacker News titles with the analysis based on Watson Natural Language Understanding*

Your app is only a simple example, but you can take it further and develop it to the full functionality, like the one that is also open sourced and called "Hackers."[6]

Summary

Congratulations! You have completed the first full mobile app with Serverless Mobile Backend-as-a-Service. You have used fanning out and fanning in patterns on some scale. Now you are ready to learn more about use cases beyond what you have used here – AI-based data processing. In the next chapter, there are described eight use cases you might see the most relevant in conjunction with Serverless. Keep on reading.

---

[6]https://github.com/weiran/Hackers

CHAPTER 7

Use Cases

As you may have inferred in previous chapters, there are many potentially valuable reasons to use Serverless technology in your next project. In this chapter, you will discover eight typical use cases or patterns for Serverless Swift applications. Our feeling is that with these use cases, you will be able to quickly understand when and how to apply Serverless Swift in real-life situations.

Use cases as a concept made its entry on to the software market in the early 1990s thanks to the Swedish computer scientist Ivar Jacobson. Jacobson's insight was that it was important to clearly document the role the various actors played in a software program. He wanted to document in plain English what the actors were trying to accomplish and the role they were playing and then design the program around the actors and their activities.

The eight use cases we present in this chapter describe the various architectural alternatives a designer has when Serverless technologies are applied to solve problem domains. This chapter in many ways is a good place to start reading this book. Here you are presented with a series of code patterns that you can easily modify to create a successful solution to an architectural problem, using serverless computing.

It is important to mention that the first common component of most of these cases is the IBM API Gateway. It serves as a funnel into the IBM Cloud backend. The IBM API Gateway is the central piece that connects the IBM Cloud with the outside world.

© Marek Sadowski and Lennart Frantzell 2020
M. Sadowski and L. Frantzell, *Serverless Swift*,
https://doi.org/10.1007/978-1-4842-5836-1_7

Behind the IBM API Gateway, you find IBM Cloud Functions – managed Apache OpenWhisk in IBM Cloud – the IBM core technology of the Serverless Functions that will do the heavy lifting in the presented eight use cases. Another key component is the Software-as-a-Service that provides persistent storage for data in a form of records, files, streams, or messages.

With just those three software components, API Gateway, IBM Cloud Functions, and SaaS-based storage or a Cloud-based system, you have the triangular code pattern that you will be able to bend and change ad infinitum to create simple but powerful solutions to problems you want to solve with light-way Serverless technology.

In the following sections, you are going to investigate the typical use cases and examples for Serverless backends, Mobile Serverless Backends: the data processing use case, the AI data processing use case, the IoT use case, the events stream processing, the chatbot or conversational scenarios, and finally scheduled, that is, crone-like tasks. You can jump to any interesting use case for your particular situation or just begin with the first use case, Serverless backends.

Serverless backends

In addition to the comfort without the need for management and operations of the SaaS, a Cloud backend is used to store, manipulate, and retrieve the information from a globally accessible "storage." You can find the architecture of this basic use case in Figure 7-1.

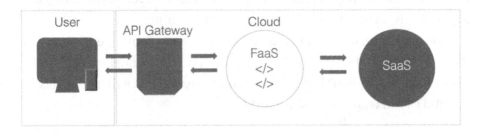

Figure 7-1. *Serverless backend*

If you look closer into this pattern, you will realize that in most cases a full set of CRUD operations – meaning Create, Read, Update, and finally the Delete operations – would be needed for your API. These operations implemented as actions could be neatly packaged together using IBM Cloud Functions/Apache OpenWhisk and offered up for reuse. In a microservice instead of calling various basic exposed Serverless actions by themselves, you would rather see them gathered together. Such an approach is possible by using the API Gateway.

Note   The inclusion of an API Gateway with OpenWhisk enables you to easily expose your *actions* as RESTful endpoints. While Serverless actions are designed to represent just a single function, either Create or Read, you often find a need to create an API proxy that could offer you with the full function set for RESTful microservice.

The microservice, represented by the RESTful API, allowing for usage with the entire CRUD operations, and documented with Swagger or OpenAPI, is something particularly useful, since being de facto a standard and an expected facet of the Cloud native functionality. You can also assign actions to specific endpoints and even have verbs (get, put, post, delete) from the same endpoint assigned to different actions. You can already consume OpenWhisk actions from other applications using the JavaScript or iOS/Swift client SDKs. And now the API Gateway gives you an easy path to expose your OpenWhisk actions to other non-credentialed applications in order to obscure your particular Serverless architecture from the outside world and conform to the application development standards you could leverage and use for this the API Gateway.

Often you would have functions for each of your HTTP endpoints in a CRUD application. For example, imagine a conference schedule application. There will be two different approaches you can expose your actions with the API Gateway. One approach would be based on assigning

149

the API endpoint/verb combinations to specific actions individually, while the other would rely on using a Swagger config file to map API endpoints to Serverless actions. If you plan to share your APIs with other developers, you would go with the latter.

Furthermore, there are other important reasons for using the API Gateway. Now with API Gateway, it is much easier to add and edit the security aspects of the API key, the API secret, and OAuth validation. You can also enable cross-origin resource sharing (CORS) for the API Gateway to handle all CORS requests for an API.

In addition, you can fine-tune other aspects of the API usage like rate-limiting, mapping actions to API endpoints (OpenAPI Doc creation). In the API economy, the ability to share the API is the key asset for easy promotion and socialization of a product or service API. Using Serverless, you can easily share it, switch out versions and implementations, and eventually sunset it without modifications to your original Serverless APIs and their actions. Also, it is fairly easy to generate an API key for a particular user or a group allowing control of different access control for different APIs to the same service. Finally, the API Gateway provides you with more detailed analytics and offers statistics like number of API calls, errors, and response times. The IBM Cloud Functions even provides an API Explorer to quickly test your APIs as they would be used by HTTP clients.

Using ICF, the API Gateway cost is included in the same single price for execution time and can give you great control over access, and its compatibility with OpenAPI can help you set up an API from declarative specifications.

In fact, you may find that SaaS offerings may be created or extended to other users through APIs easily created and managed as part of the inherent API support included with the Apache OpenWhisk serverless platform. In some cases, it might be a database offered over the Cloud and managed by its vendor or an object storage system and so on.

Mobile Backends

Mobile devices are becoming more and more powerful. But still it is impossible to beat the power of the Cloud or Internet *compute* as subject matter experts call the entirety of its CPUs and managed data of the Cloud or Internet. Therefore, mobile devices are first to rely on the vast Internet and Cloud resources. Plenty of large applications are having its user interface on mobile devices. Sometimes there is solely a mobile user interface for some of the applications that are designed for so-called mobile first use. When the mobile application user base is small or users or applications are accessing Cloud on the event base, that is an indication for a designer to leverage the second use case, which is offering the Mobile Serverless Backend. In this approach, it is possible for mobile developers to easily access server-side logic and to outsource compute-intensive tasks to a scalable Cloud platform. Let developers implement functions in languages of their mobile platforms like Swift and easily consume server-side functions using Apache OpenWhisk iOS SDK. Figure 7-2 represents this use case.

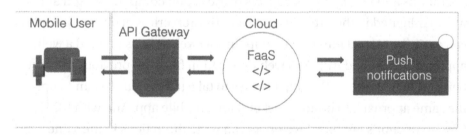

Figure 7-2. *Mobile Serverless Backend-as-a-Service*

This use case is very similar to the general Serverless backend use case, but with the addition of a push notification callback to a mobile app running on a smartphone of the user. This is an iconic use case, in that it helps to define mobile architecture. And it is worth restating that this and several of the other use cases really define major segments of society such as mobile computing, which would never have been possible without this use case. Because via push notification today, the modern society of the world receives the news.

In particular, you could imagine a process in which a news channel app owner wants to send a broadcast alert to all users about an upcoming storm, a bad air quality. And with the help of push notifications, the app owner can quickly send notifications to all the users with the storm alert, using a simple graphical user interface with just a few clicks.

As you have learned in this book, the Cloud-based functionality with Serverless technology is particularly easy and fast to implement, especially when you can use the same language such as Swift for your entire server-side development stack. This language continuity is the most sought-after feature for the mobile developers wishing to expand their development from a mobile environment into full-stack development including the Cloud and backend elements. This also allows a developer to focus on the mobile app functionality and diminish concerns over operations and management encountered with traditional Cloud development. Indeed, Serverless technology is so attractive as it takes care of all the operations and management aspects of the Cloud component. And as it was highlighted in the previous use case, the Serverless actions you deploy can easily be turned into HTTP endpoints as web actions to build a web application backend API. As a web application from the previous use case being a client to the REST API, it is easy to take it a step further and apply the same approach to build a backend for a mobile app. And with IBM Cloud Functions, mobile developers can write the actions in the same language used for their mobile app in Swift for iOS or in Java for Android.

Note   It is worth to note here that implementation of the Serverless Actions is independent from the client that is calling them. So you could easily develop Serverless Actions in Swift and then call them from an Android app that was written in Java or JavaScript.

Data processing

For the content management applications in the industrial scale for a corporation or in smaller amounts for a small startup, it is great to automate the basic processing of data to simplify your operations. Using event providers and feeds, whenever there is an insert, delete, or any change of your data in the data store, your Serverless functions can be triggered to automate various file processes, for example, for audio normalization, image rotation, picture sharpening, noise reduction, thumbnail generation, video transcoding, and so on.

We live in the digital age, and managing the amount of data being now created and made available is a challenge in itself. Application development needs to plan for the ability to process these large volumes of new data as soon as they are being made available and be able to react to it immediately. This requirement often includes processing both structured database records and unstructured documents, images, or videos. Apache OpenWhisk Serverless Actions can be configured by system-provided or custom feeds to react to changes in data and automatically trigger actions for the incoming feeds of data. Actions can be programmed to process changes, transform data formats, send and receive messages, invoke other actions, and update various data stores. As you have learned in the previous chapters, the supported data stores include SQL-based relational databases, in-memory data grids, NoSQL database, files, messaging brokers, and various other systems. Serverless action's rules and sequences provide flexibility to change the processing pipeline without programming. The setup of the process can be done easily through simple configuration updates. The various available data store feeds and easy configuration make an OpenWhisk-based system highly agile and easily adaptable to changing requirements.

You can find the architecture of the use case in Figure 7-3.

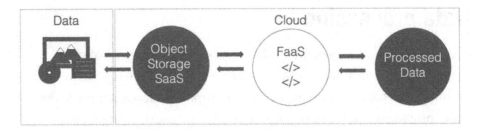

Figure 7-3. *Data processing*

AI data processing

The use case for data processing has a significant branch of use involving AI-based services. And this becomes on its own another iconic use case that defines a whole new social movement: the use of AI in society. In addition to typical processing of data, as soon as it becomes available, you might want to create a Serverless action that makes use of powerful AI services like IBM Watson to detect objects or people appearing in images or videos, transcribe audio to text with the Speech-to-Text AI service, or analyze the tone of messages as they are being generated by systems and people and so on.

AI-based services can be effectively combined with Apache OpenWhisk to create powerful applications. For example, Watson Visual Recognition can be used with OpenWhisk to automatically extract useful information from videos without having to watch them. This AI-based technology is the "cognitive" extension of the data processing use case that was discussed earlier. See Figure 7-4 with the typical setup of the AI data processing.

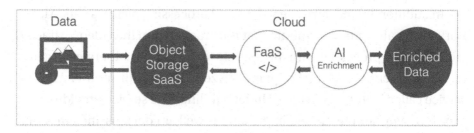

Figure 7-4. *AI-based data enrichment*

One of the open source examples that you might want to base your future development on is the Dark Vision AI data processing application which development was led and done mainly by authors' colleague Frederic Lavigne[1] at IBM. The Dark Vision application deals with the processing and tagging of numerous videos made available online or simply from your company repository. A user would upload a video or an image by using the Dark Vision web application. The web component would store the data asset in the SaaS data storage (think of the S3-compliant object storage or a NoSQL database). Once the video is uploaded, with the help of the feeds based on the data storage, the trigger is fired as soon as the change is detected. The trigger launches the video extractor action. This action implements the data processing use case. The video is being processed by the video extractor action, and it generates still frames that are loaded back to the object storage. Each frame appearance in the data storage triggers another action – that in this instance implements the AI data processing use case. The AI enrichment action gets each of the pictures and analyzes it with AI Visual Recognition service. The resulting tags with the description of the observed objects and their classifications are then stored in the database associating them with the uploaded video.

---

[1]The Dark Vision GitHub repository – a good example, but archived:
https://github.com/IBM-Cloud/openwhisk-darkvisionapp

155

In addition to transforming videos and processing pictures with AI, Dark Vision also processes audio that is extracted from the video. Extracted audio is being processed with the Speech-to-Text AI-based service to get the text transcript. This transcript is analyzed further with another AI service called Natural Language Understanding. The service provides keywords, entities mentioned in the text, as well as concepts and emotions. Thanks to all these elements, you could have a rough idea what the movie is about and the mood of dialogs.

Note   You might want to analyze with Dark Vision[2] – an OpenWhisk-based service – both the infrequent video blogs of your favorite blogger and get the heavy load processed efficiently in the enterprise setup when obtaining a large video library for content analysis, object tagging, and dialogs. Think about all the videos individuals and companies (media and entertainment) accumulate every year. How can you keep track of what's inside of them so you can quickly search and find what you're looking for? "Show me all the videos that have Arc De Triomphe in it" or "Show me all the videos that talk about peaches." What if we used artificial intelligence to process these videos to tell us which video has what we're looking for without us having to watch all of them?

Internet of Things and Edge ready

Internet of Things (IoT) or novel Edge-based scenarios are often inherently sensor-driven. For example, an action in OpenWhisk might be triggered if there is a need to react to an event originating from a sensor with a

---

[2]https://github.com/IBM-Cloud/openwhisk-darkvisionapp

message that a specific temperature is exceeded. IoT interactions are usually stateless with the potential of the high load in major spontaneous events such as natural disasters, significant weather storms, or traffic jams. There is a demand for an elastic system that has a small normal workload, but it might need to scale quickly with predictable response time. Therefore, the ability to handle many simultaneous events with no prior warning to the system is desirable. It is not economically viable to build and manage an oversized system to meet these high-end requirements using traditional server architectures. As such, the dedicated systems tend to be over-provisioned and highly expensive – or alternatively underpowered and unable to handle peak loads, when they are really needed.

Moreover, IoT applications use the combination of different services and data bridges. And these services and bridges require high performance and flexible pipelines that are spanning from IoT devices up to Cloud storage and an analytics platform. Often pre-configured bridges lack the programmability to implement and fine-tune a particular solution architecture. Given the variety of pipelines and the lack of standardization around data fusion in general (IoT in particular), it is common to see environments where the pipeline requires custom data transformation. These custom data transformations apply to format conversion, filtering, or augmentation. OpenWhisk is an excellent tool to implement such a transformation, in a Serverless manner, where the custom logic is hosted on a fully managed and elastic Cloud platform. You can refer to the typical architecture of such the IoT-based use case presented in Figure 7-5.

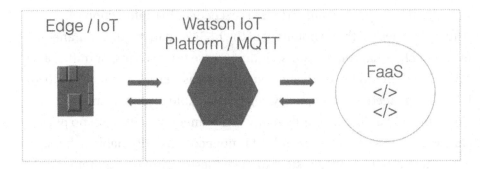

Figure 7-5. Edge and IoT ready

Note   You can quickly find that the Internet of Things is the cornerstone of a large number of use cases around IBM's Internet of Things platform. IBM's Internet of Things platform is hosted on the IBM Cloud along with the managed Apache OpenWhisk as IBM Cloud Functions.

The IBM IoT platform can react to and process IoT sensor data. IoT devices send data to the IBM Watson IoT platform which defines Cloud rules on how to call your Serverless functions and execute custom application logic.

Because of Lennart's interest and expertise in Blockchain, he prefers the following example for this generic use case to be in the Edge and Blockchain space:[3] "You might want to develop a system for ocean going ships that are loaded with shipping containers equipped with IoT devices that can send temperature data to Blockchain's Smart Contracts. IoT devices can communicate with Smart Contracts that can verify that the relative humidity (RH) inside the container remains in the range between

---

[3]www.ibm.com/blogs/blockchain/2019/06/blockchain-and-iot-in-commercial-transportation/

40 and 50 percent. A sensor which is mounted inside the container monitors the RH and communicates the data to the smart Bill of Lading (BoL) in real-time. In the case of the ocean waves overflowing the hull or when the weather is just poor and the humidity level goes to an unacceptable level inside containers, the BoL is automatically breached and concerned parties are notified at the same time. The smart contract then triggers a payment or force compensation to the aggrieved party."

Marek's preference is in the automation of waste disposal and its monitoring for smart cities. The entire solution is based on a device which collects information regarding every waste bin pickup.[4] The information which is being collected includes time, location, and bin capacity. The raw data regarding every pickup is encapsulated in a file which is transmitted via sFTP to the Cloud, while the truck's location and status is transmitted using MQTT to the Watson IoT platform. Every file and every MQTT message being uploaded to the Cloud trigger OpenWhisk actions, for instance, to insert information into a report database and to start ongoing monitoring algorithms that create alerts. The analyzed information regarding the waste collection is stored in the database, while every API call or the UI access triggers an action for fetching the relevant data from the database, analyzing it and making the information available via an API or the UI.

To conclude, smart city solutions that must maintain a high level of service to their clients would profit more from this unique approach of OpenWhisk. Smart waste collection providers or city governors could be sure that they would be working in smarter and more efficient ways without having to handle scalability and computing power issues.

---

[4]https://medium.com/openwhisk/openwhisk-for-a-smart-city-data-application-dccd7894e0e1

Event stream processing

One of the popular use cases in Cloud-based computing is processing of event streams. There are times when computer programs perform the synchronous call return between threads. Yet there is often a need for asynchronous calls. In such a situation, a program passes information to a queue in another address space and does not wait for a return message. Instead, such a program simply continues on its merry way, leaving it to others to pop the message off the queue to decipher it. There are lots of software that work with asynchronous queues and stacks. You might be familiar with solutions based on the Message-Oriented Middleware such as IBM MQ, Java Message Service, Oracle Message Service, Redis, and others.

Message queues provide an asynchronous communications protocol. This protocol allows the sender and receiver of the message to not interact with the message queue at the same time. Messages placed onto the queue are stored until the recipient retrieves them. The specific implementations of queue-based middleware define implicit or explicit limits on the size of data that may be transmitted in a single message. Queues also typically allow you to configure the number of messages that may remain outstanding on the queue and how you wish to persist the messages.

In recent years Apache Kafka, an Apache open source project, has become extremely popular and is today a staple of many leading software products. Apache Kafka was originally developed by LinkedIn and was open sourced in early 2011 and then graduated from the Apache Incubator in 2012. It is named after the immortal author Franz Kafka.

Since there are often situations, when there are events – and eventually Serverless actions – that are originating from Kafka streams of messages, the popularity of this implementation has led to the creation of the pattern and eventually to a generic use case. You can review Figure 7-6 that is showing this particular event stream processing use case.

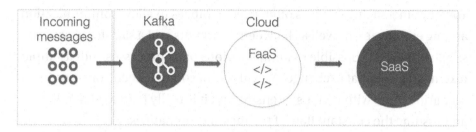

Figure 7-6. *Processing event streams with Kafka*

The possibility to trigger OpenWhisk actions with Kafka records became very simple thanks to the OpenWhisk feed package dedicated to this project: `https://github.com/apache/openwhisk-package-kafka`.

It is worth noting that you can find the managed Kafka project in IBM Cloud, where it is called IBM Event Streams. IBM Cloud Functions is ideal to be used with Kafka or IBM Event Streams and other messaging middleware. The event-driven nature of those systems requires an event-driven runtime to process messages. The runtime can apply business logic to those messages, which is exactly what Cloud Functions provides, with its feeds, triggers, and actions.

Kafka and Event Streams are often used for high and highly irregular or unpredictable workload volumes. Thanks to ready-made integrations using ICF, Serverless action-based consumers of those messages can be easily created and reactively scale on a moment's notice. As you have learned in the previous sections, Cloud Functions has built-in capability to consume messages as well as publish messages that are provided in the Event Streams package.

Conversational scenarios

Another great use case is connected with the social messaging services. You might find the chatbots serving various purposes in many web pages or applications both representing Fortune 500 companies and startups.

You have messaging services often used in offices to allow communication among employees, as well as between customers and a salesforce or a support. Now it is possible to initiate various bank processes with a simple text message or chat exchange. As with event streams, such conversational scenarios come with various intensity, and it is really hard to generalize and assume the constant flow of the message exchanges.

In general, Serverless actions seem a great technology to be used to connect messaging services with the backends. With OpenWhisk, it became fairly easy to implement serverless conversational applications, like chatbots, for example, with Slack messaging service, or Facebook Messenger, by passing chat messages to your functions for further processing, thanks to the intermediary connectivity over the chatbot backbone using IBM Watson Assistant and its Slack or Facebook Messenger packages. See Figure 7-7 for the details.

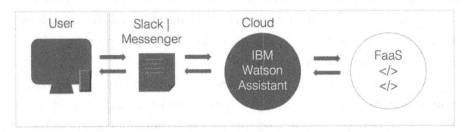

Figure 7-7. *Integration with Slack or Facebook Messenger*

In the simplest scenario of creating a Slackbot and connecting a Slack to the Cloud-based SaaS storage or a database, you would start with connecting IBM Watson Assistant to the messaging platform like Slack or Facebook Messenger service. Your bot based on the Slack service is backed then by the IBM Watson Assistant service. You will integrate Slack and IBM Watson Assistant using an Assistant integration. In the event of the need of invoking a Serverless Action, you would trigger the IBM Cloud Functions' web action. You can use a webhook in the Watson Assistant to call a Cloud Functions action that is secured. For more information, see "Calling an IBM Cloud Functions web action."[5]

The entire flow would then include the Slack integration channels messages between Slack and Watson Assistant. There, some server-side dialog actions might perform, for example, SQL queries against a Cloud-based database.

Scheduled tasks

The scheduled tasks use case could be the first use case as the strength of serverless is cost savings for aperiodic usage patterns where servers/hosting costs are avoided.

This is typically the first use case adopted for those transitioning from legacy systems looking to save on IT budget and right up there with API management use cases.

Scheduled events are Cloud native events you can programmatically control when they need to be fired to run your serverless apps, instead of allocating an idle server just to schedule a job.

You can use IBM Cloud Functions to orchestrate your applications using these types of triggers – see Figure 7-8 for details.

---

[5]https://cloud.ibm.com/docs/assistant?topic=assistant-dialog-webhooks#dialog-webhooks-cf-web-action

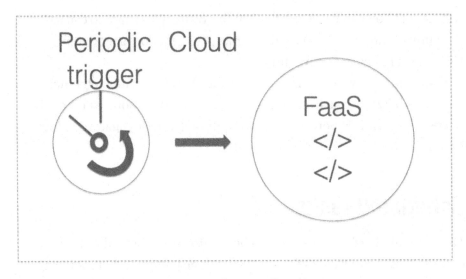

Figure 7-8. *Running actions with Periodic triggers*

There are three major types of alarms that you can use to schedule your Actions. They are described in the following sections.

Interval-based triggers

This type of a trigger can be used in Continuous Deployment and Operations such as monitoring and health tests. You can configure an action to run every set amount of minutes.

Fire-once-based triggers

In some cases, actions are meant to run once. These actions are usually created programmatically from your serverless apps to continue with a task or invoke a final Action at some point in the future. Or perhaps you just want to send a personalized social message to every family member at exactly midnight on New Year's Eve!

CRON-based triggers

The CRON-based trigger event was the first trigger available as soon as the periodic event-based Actions were introduced. Developers wanted more control on when the trigger starts to fire and when it stops. This type of trigger was recently enhanced with two new options to handle start and stop dates. You can learn more about how to use these two new options in the Cloud Functions documentation.

Note   CRON-based trigger was improved to handle start and stop dates. At the time of writing this book, these enhancements are available only via the Cloud Functions CLI plug-in. Read more about it here: `www.ibm.com/cloud/blog/new-alarm-based-trigger-events-for-ibm-cloud-functions`.

Summary

With the generalized use cases described earlier, you are now equipped with a set of well-rounded scenarios that you can implement in your next project. You can easily defend your architecture by referring to the most applied industry use cases. In the next section, you are going to find out about a couple additional in-depth strategies that would allow you expose your functions in the API economy context and your functions to prevail and overcome typical limits imposed by managed Serverless platforms. Keep on reading!

CHAPTER 8

Cloud Native Development Best Practices

From the previous chapters, you amassed a good amount of knowledge on how to use Serverless technology. The current chapter will give you practical tips on how to adjust your development strategies to deal with the limits imposed by Apache OpenWhisk services or the vendors offering you Cloud-based OpenWhisk, like IBM Cloud Functions.

You will also find some helpful advice for deploying an enterprise-grade serverless application in the Cloud. There is a set of best deployment practices that you should be aware of and that are connected with security aspects of application deployment. Additionally, there are considerations for using the API Gateway for fencing your Serverless actions from the outside and monetizing your APIs by using IBM API Connect which provides more authorization options. Also, this chapter offers strategies on avoiding long "cold" start times with Serverless Swift functions and ways to "warm" them up, including the use of Docker-based containers, and dealing with business transactions by implementing server-side Swift applications.

Finally, you can find a basic overview of the Cloud providers that are offering Apache OpenWhisk for Serverless functionality.

© Marek Sadowski and Lennart Frantzell 2020
M. Sadowski and L. Frantzell, *Serverless Swift*,
https://doi.org/10.1007/978-1-4842-5836-1_8

Security aspects and IAM

Cloud security is becoming more important and at the same time more complicated as Public Clouds diverge into Public Clouds, Private Clouds, Multi Clouds, and Hybrid Clouds.

Many Cloud service providers have their own Cloud security policies, user access, and connectivity, which, unless you are up to date with the very latest Cloud security policies, can leave you open to security breaches or non-compliant workloads.

One particular service, called IAM, provides developers in this space with much needed security functionality. Identity and access management (IAM) in enterprise IT does, as the term implies, deal with defining and managing the roles and access privileges of network users. The core objective of IAM systems is securing and maintaining one digital identity per individual. IAM is best when working so much in sync with the day-to-day operations of the business that users don't even realize it's there. And because of that fact, the IAM Cloud service is very useful for Serverless developers.

While some approaches to IAM can force security in front of the user, silent security works better when working quietly in the background, providing the right levels of access to the right users.

When using IBM Cloud Functions in IBM Cloud, the IBM IAM service adds authentication, privileged access management, identity governance, and access management solutions. IAM also grants access rights, provides your Serverless-based applications with single sign-on, working from any device, enhancing the security with multi-factor authentication, enabling your user lifecycle management, and protecting privileged accounts in the enterprise-grade way. See Figure 8-1 for the screenshot.

Figure 8-1. *IAM-based services that are discussed in this chapter*

Privileged access management

The term Identity-as-a-Service (IDaaS) refers to Cloud-based identity and access management (IAM) solutions that help control user access to resources from a hosted environment.[1] The key benefit of IDaaS is speed. When you can provide simpler, faster management tools for deploying IT resources to users, your business can adopt new technology more quickly.

Whether you are looking for a secure bridge to Cloud IAM or a transformative makeover of your identity environment, IBM Cloud-based offerings can deliver a business-friendly IAM. One of those offerings that you might use to manage and authenticate users is the App ID service. IAM framework integrates seamlessly with IBM Cloud Functions and the App ID service.

The IBM Cloud documentation offers a full example detailing usage of App ID service with an iOS mobile app with IBM Cloud Functions iOS SDK and IBM Cloud Functions backend with the callback done with mobile notification service.[2] The actions developed in Swift can be found in the following GitHub repository: `https://github.com/IBM-Cloud/ serverless-followupapp-ios`.

---

[1]`https://cloud.ibm.com/docs/openwhisk?topic=cloud-functions-iam`
[2]`https://cloud.ibm.com/docs/solution-tutorials?topic=solution- tutorials-serverless-mobile-backend&programming_ language=swift#serverless-mobile-backend`

API Gateway

As you have discovered in the previous chapters, IBM Cloud API Gateway is a free service that you can use to create, secure, share, and manage APIs that access IBM Cloud resources.[3] API Gateway clearly distinguishes IBM Cloud Functions – Apache OpenWhisk – and its implementations for web actions from the Serverless competition. The API Gateway works by inserting a fast and lightweight gateway in front of existing IBM Cloud endpoints. The gateway intercepts incoming API calls, executes security policies, and then routes the call to the backend application. After the request is processed, the backend application sends the response to the gateway, which then routes it back to the caller.

The API Gateway offers you important features such as **rate limiting**, which is one of the protections from abusive over-usage of the APIs. You can enforce a rate limit to manage the number of calls that applications can make to your APIs. You can specify a rate limit so that only a permitted number of calls are made per second, minute, or hour. You can set this rate to apply to the overall API or set a single limit for the API that applies to a particular API key.

Furthermore, by using API Gateway's OAuth capabilities, you can prevent unauthorized access to your data. Moreover, you can also ensure that only users with the correct authentication can access your APIs. The OAuth token-based authorization protocol allows third-party websites or applications to access user data without requiring the user to share personal information.

As we mentioned in Chapter 7, you can enable cross-origin resource sharing (CORS) as the mechanism that uses HTTP headers to allow an app to retrieve data from an API across domain boundaries. Only those cross-domain API calls that include the appropriate CORS header can be

---

[3]https://developer.ibm.com/patterns/serverless-microservices-api-gateway/

fulfilled. If your API does not enable CORS, then it can return data only to apps within the same domain.

Finally, API analytics provides you with additional features based on the LogDNA service (`www.ibm.com/cloud/log-analysis`) to store and display information that is generated during API invocations. You can use the analytics feature to track call usage. You can also monitor usage to understand how your APIs are being used so that you can make informed decisions about how to update your APIs to increase adoption.

API Gateway fencing

A great use case described in the previous chapter with the Serverless backend use case is to have functions for each of your HTTP endpoints in a CRUD application. The API Gateway cost is included in the same single price for execution time and can give you great control over access, and its compatibility with OpenAPI can help you set up an API from a declarative spec.

When a request arrives at the API Gateway, the gateway routes the request to the target API and runs the API to access the backend resources that are made available through the API. The API Gateway also allows you to monitor API activities and perform analytics based on the activity data. The API Gateway supports REST APIs that are compliant with version 2.0 of the Swagger specification.

For example, imagine a conference schedule application. First, you would define the Serverless actions using IBM Cloud Functions named like "getUser", "createUser", or "deleteUser". Then you would map API endpoints in the API Gateway for GET, POST, and DELETE to respective Actions. Refer to Figure 8-2 to see the visualization of this scenario available also in IBM Cloud documentation.[4]

---

[4]`https://cloud.ibm.com/docs/tutorials?topic=solution-tutorials-serverless-api-webapp`

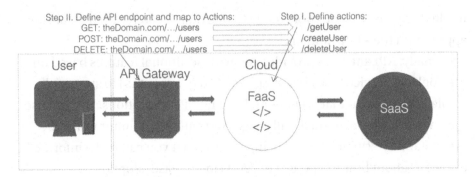

Figure 8-2. *API Gateway abstracts away Serverless functions*

Multi-region deployments with Serverless functions

IBM Cloud Functions technology is available in multiple IBM Cloud locations dedicated to various geographic regions. To increase resiliency and reduce network latency, applications can deploy their backend in multiple locations. And with the help of IBM Cloud Internet Services (CIS), developers can expose a single entry point in charge of distributing traffic to the closest healthy backend. Refer to Figure 8-3.

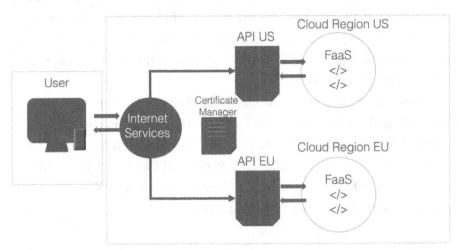

Figure 8-3. *Cloud Internet Services redirects requests to the closest Cloud Functions engine*

From the entry point, users access the application. Their requests go through IBM Cloud Internet Services. IBM Cloud Internet Services redirects the requests to the closest healthy API backend. In addition to CIS, you need to provide the SSL certificate to encrypt the route end to end. For this purpose, you need to provision the Certificate Manager that is also available in IBM Cloud. It provides your API with its SSL certificate and allows for end-to-end encryption of the entire traffic. Finally, the API endpoints are mapped to implemented functions with Cloud Functions. There are several references available that show this example in more details – you can use both the tutorials and patterns.[5]

API Connect for billing, and further authorization

If you start to think to monetize your API and start billing for its usage, you need something more than just API Gateway. The product dedicated to the API economy, sharing, discovery, and monetizing of the APIs is IBM API Connect. API Connect is a scalable API platform that lets you create, expose, manage, and monetize APIs across Clouds. It includes a single, signed, encrypted gateway, which greatly reduces your risk of a cybersecurity incident. With it, you can publish APIs in its dedicated API Portal and offer various plans from the free Plans for your customers to use your products; you can also define Plans that automatically bill your customers who are using your APIs.

Many companies have started billing customers for the use of their APIs as an additional revenue stream. With API Connect for IBM Cloud, you can configure billing subscriptions for members who have access to your Developer Portal and credit card billing that automatically processes through a credit card processing service account.

---

[5]www.ibm.com/cloud/blog/load-balancing-api-calls-across-regions-with-ibm-cloud-internet-services-and-cloud-api-gateway (a blogpost); https://cloud.ibm.com/docs/solution-tutorials?topic=solution-tutorials-multi-region-serverless#multi-region-serverless (a tutorial).

When you make your APIs available to your customers on your API Connect for IBM Cloud Developer Portal, you assign them one or more Plans that define the terms of use for the APIs.

You can define free Plans and billing Plans. Your customers might have different needs for the use of the APIs, so you can offer different levels of service. An example of this is a smaller customer that only needs a rate of 5 API calls per hour.

A larger company might need a rate of 1000 API calls per hour. Since the smaller customer does not want to pay the same amount as the larger company for fewer calls, they can subscribe to a more limited Plan.

Though much of the procedure is the same for setting up a billing Plan and a free Plan, there are some extra actions that you need to complete when you define billing Plans.

There are various resources to be used to learn more. Find them here:

- `https://cloud.ibm.com/docs/`
  `apiconnect?topic=apiconnect-creating_apis`

- `http://jamesthom.as/blog/2016/04/26/serverless-`
  `apis-with-openwhisk-and-api-connect/`

Cold–warm start of Serverless Swift functions

When you start your journey with Serverless Swift, you will notice the significant difference between cold and warm call responses from IBM Cloud Functions written in Swift. This section would give you a couple strategies on dealing with it and improving the response times, by pre-warming the functions and compiling them before deployment.

Pre-warming for cold starts

As you know the *cold start* refers to starting the CPU from power off, without any existing configurations or software installed or loaded. The same thing occurs in Serverless and implementations such as Apache OpenWhisk. The cold start refers to starting a Container on a virtual CPU without any of your action code or its dependencies loaded. Specifically, serverless cold start refers to the time needed to load the Swift stack and your function and its dependencies before they are available for invocation. Suffering cold start affects the ability of your swift functions to quickly process event data or respond to APIs to the first caller. The first cold-start response to the calls might even take several seconds, while subsequent "warm" calls are delivered in a couple dozen milliseconds.

Serverless cold-start times are a special consideration for Swift developers when using OpenWhisk. The information in the OpenWhisk documentation explains that "when you create a Swift action with a Swift source file, it has to be compiled into a binary before the action is run. Once done, subsequent calls to the action are much faster until the container that holds your action is purged. This delay is known as the cold-start delay." This expensive startup latency (called the "cold-start" latency) is incurred by the *swiftc* compiler. Using the CLI for a blocking invoke which returns the full activation record, the time spent executing the action is stored in the duration property. The activation for *helloSwift* took ~3 seconds. Invoking the action again, you can see that the action benefits from a "warm start" and the activation is much faster (<30 milliseconds).

Another definition states that *warm start* refers to restarting the CPU without first turning the power off. Program processing starts once again where retentive data is retained without turning the power off. Similarly, in your case in order to make the Swift Cloud Functions actions performant every single time and avoiding cold-start delay, we need to use some strategy for that. And the recipe by the OpenWhisk documentation is this: "To avoid the cold-start delay, you can compile your Swift file into a binary and then upload to Cloud Functions in a zip file. As you need the OpenWhisk scaffolding, the easiest way to create the binary is to build it within the same environment it runs in." So your goal would be to precompile the binary and use it to run a Swift action. Doing so you would drop the expensive compilation step and get the execution time of the action to be closer to the warm start.

In order to develop such a precompiled package, you would also need Docker to run the Swift action container locally. Docker will allow you to build the binary in the same environment as requested in the preceding recipe. Also you will be required to manage the Swift version with Docker, according to what is being used in the Cloud. Basically, you need to download the Docker Desktop for macOS, or Windows, or apt-get Docker for your Linux distro.

After launching the Docker image with the desired Swift distro and copying the action source file, you might optionally want to also add needed libraries to your Package.swift file. After compiling your action and the zip process, you will find the <action>.zip. So now, you need to only update your action with the zip and try by calling the action.[6]

Alternative approach without the complexity of Docker

Alternatively, you might want to simply pre-warm the action calling it yourself when you update it. Then there would be only the challenge in keeping it warm between calls and after the first call.

---

[6]www.ibm.com/cloud/blog/performant-swift-serverless-actions and https://cloud.ibm.com/docs/openwhisk?topic=openwhisk-prep#prep_swift42_multi

Staying warm

Another challenge accented in the preceding section is that the warmed up actions stay warm only for about 5 minutes in the IBM Cloud Functions. This is a strategy being implemented by most of the Serverless providers to keep their system resources at bay. So you will again need to wait extra time, if the call to your Serverless backend comes after the specified 5 minutes. If that is something you would like to avoid, you would need to create a CRON action that would call your Serverless every 5 minutes to keep it warm.

Docker and server-side Swift for business transaction support

As you have discovered in the previous chapters while serverless is good for many situations, it is not good for every situation. There are a number of cases in which you would fall back to the traditional HA-based architectures especially for long-running processes or in order to be able to migrate the system efficiently among the Clouds.

As it comes to long-running processes, as you already know that FaaS Serverless workloads are designed to scale up and down perfectly in response to workload, offering significant cost savings for spiky workloads. But for workloads characterized by long-running processes, at the given average transaction levels, the same cost advantages are no longer present and managing a traditional server environment might be simpler, more predictable, and more cost-effective.

In respect to the vendor lock-in, there is not a common standard in the Serverless architectures as of now. And these Serverless architectures are designed to take advantage of an ecosystem of managed Cloud services and, in terms of architectural models, go the furthest to decouple a workload from something more portable, like a VM or a container.

For some companies, deeply integrating with the native managed services of Cloud providers is where much of the value of Cloud can be found; for other organizations, these patterns represent material lock-in risks that need to be mitigated.

In the previous section, you learned some workarounds to make the Swift Serverless actions pre-warmed, but still the cold starts are the biggest challenge for some. And because Serverless architectures forgo long-running processes in favor of scaling up and down to zero, they also sometimes need to start up from zero to serve a new request. For certain applications, this delay isn't much of an impact, but for something like a low-latency financial application, this delay wouldn't be acceptable. For those later types, you need to take advantage of a traditional approach of an application server that is ready for your requests. See Figure 8-4.

When you need to really know the fine-tuning of your application environment and you are tasked with monitoring and debugging, these operational tasks are challenging in any distributed system, and the move to both microservices and serverless architectures (and the combination of the two) has only exacerbated the complexity associated with managing these environments carefully.

Another consideration is that there are limits on the duration and size of the functions and their payloads – and transactions that are longer might risk timing out after 10 seconds or exceeding the limit on the size (function can have less than couple hundred of MB) would need to allow other infrastructure components in the traditional setup to take such the workload. Since serverless is stateless, you also need to consider how to maintain the state of the function that relies on SaaS-based resources (DBs, storage, etc.). Therefore, you may need to use the Docker container approach in order to increase the size of the action you need to use with your Apache OpenWhisk actions.[7]

---

[7]https://github.com/apache/openwhisk-runtime-docker

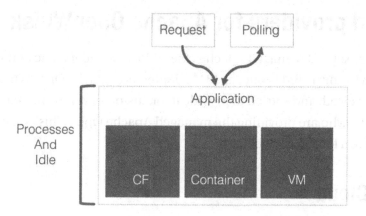

Figure 8-4. *When the traditional model is a better choice*

In order to expand the limits of size of your application or technologies being used, you would use Docker containers. And some elements of that approach were discussed in the previous section.

For traditional implementations needed for those cases not good for Serverless approach, you can still use Swift on the server-side. There are three popular server-side swift projects that could be used here: Kitura, Vapor, and others.[8] You can find a robust book – *Server Side Swift with Kitura* written by authors' colleagues: Chris Bailey and David Okun – on using the traditional server, Kitura, that is available also in IBM Cloud. Kitura's architecture is based on the approach borrowed from the popular Express.js package. It is based on Swift and as Serverless Swift serves our purpose when the traditional approach is expected.

---

[8]www.slideshare.net/cnbailey/altconf-2019-serverside-swift-state-of-the-union

Cloud providers for Apache OpenWhisk

There are several managed Apache OpenWhisk providers. The authors decided to cover IBM Cloud, as IBM adopted the Apache OpenWhisk as it was conceived, and started to provide it for customers early on. But there are others who are providing the managed Apache OpenWhisk platform. Let's have a look at each of them.

IBM Cloud

IBM Cloud supports Apache OpenWhisk as IBM Cloud Functions (`https://cloud.ibm.com/functions/`), a polyglot Function-as-a-Service (FaaS) programming platform for developing lightweight code that scalably executes on demand. This book describes the platform in more detail.

Adobe I/O

The Adobe I/O Runtime uses Apache OpenWhisk serverless platform "under the covers" to allow you to quickly deploy custom code to respond to events and execute functions right in the Cloud, all with no server setup required.

Developers can run code on top of our Cloud solutions, bringing Adobe services together with APIs. The functions run in close proximity to the content and data already stored with Adobe, making it quick and easy to create a custom solution.

Adobe decided to build their Adobe I/O Runtime on top of Apache OpenWhisk and was an initial sponsor for the open source project when it was being incubated at the Apache Software Foundation. It is worth mentioning that Adobe is an active contributor to OpenWhisk and has created some amazing tooling for the project including the project's new "quick start" single container implementation for developers.

Nimbella

Nimbella is a pure serverless Cloud that leverages the Public Cloud infrastructure and can be extended to private on-premise infrastructure. It is built on open standards, giving developers full control over their architecture and code, without vendor lock-in.

Summary

You might want to find additional resources on the best practices, workarounds, and ways to keep up with the pace of the rushing forward Cloud-based Serverless programming. The next chapter is exactly what you need to continue further.

CHAPTER 9

Conclusions

Congratulations on completing the book. In our opinion, you should be well-equipped for your next project using Serverless Swift and Apache OpenWhisk. In this chapter, we will summarize key points, use cases, and patterns as well as provide references to further resources which may be useful in taking your next steps along the road to Serverless mastery.

Summary of topics and key takeaways

In this book, we have covered the following topics:

- **Introducing Serverless, the next generation of Cloud Computing** – Serverless as a new paradigm bypassing Infrastructure-as-a-Service and presenting a lightweight development concept to the developer community. A concept that makes it possible for small teams of developers to quickly develop substantial Cloud-based applications with a minimum amount of resources. The new lightweight programming paradigm promises to unleash a flurry of new lightweight apps that despite their ease of use can create serious applications.

© Marek Sadowski and Lennart Frantzell 2020
M. Sadowski and L. Frantzell, *Serverless Swift*,
https://doi.org/10.1007/978-1-4842-5836-1_9

- **Apache OpenWhisk, Open Source Project** – In the second chapter, you got an introduction to Apache OpenWhisk, an open source, distributed Serverless platform that executes functions in response to events at any scale. OpenWhisk manages the infrastructure, servers, and scaling using Docker containers so you can focus on building amazing and efficient applications.

- In the next three chapters, you did focus on Apache OpenWhisk: in Chapter 3, you learned about **Apache OpenWhisk** project. Then in Chapter 4, you found out on how to write your **Hello World application with Apache OpenWhisk in Swift;** and in Chapter 5, you had a **Deep Dive into Apache OpenWhisk** technology.

- You were able to experience development of **a Complete iOS app with Serverless Swift Backend** in the complete iOS app using Serverless Swift.

- Then you learned about eight popular **Use Cases** and you round it out with **Cloud Native Best Practices**.

When to use Serverless – Apache OpenWhisk – and when not to use it

Serverless computing has established itself as the go-to technology for building and running applications and services without having to concern oneself with managing servers. Serverless is an essential technology for pretty much all Cloud platforms that provide compute services and as such eliminates infrastructure and the myriad management and operational tasks associated with hardware and software servers in the Clouds that today cover the globe.

By establishing itself above the infrastructure, operating system, and language framework levels in the Cloud stack, serverless requires almost no management or operation of infrastructure from the application developer, enabling them to focus more narrowly on code, its quick and elastic deployment, and writing the custom business logic.

When to run workload on Serverless

Serverless runs code only on demand on a per-request basis, horizontally scaling transparently with the number of requests being served. In this manner, companies that utilize Serverless pay only for the resources necessary to complete actual tasks while knowing they will be used in the most efficient manner and never having to pay for idle capacity. For most applications running in the Cloud, this could end up being a very big savings indeed. For certain workloads, such as ones that require massive parallel processing, especially on an irregular basis, serverless can not only be faster but the cumulative cost-effectiveness could be enormous from traditional or dedicated alternatives.

When running Serverless is not practical

But Serverless computing can also have cons and situations when it does not fit and when it can be downright wrong to use it:

- Long-running processes – FaaS and serverless work-loads are designed to scale up and down perfectly in response to workload, offering significant cost savings for spiky workloads. But for workloads characterized by long-running processes, these same cost advantages are no longer present and managing a traditional server environment might be simpler and more cost-effective.

- Vendor lock-in – Serverless architectures are designed to take advantage of an ecosystem of managed Cloud services and, in terms of architectural models, go the furthest to decouple a workload from something more portable, like a VM or a container. For some companies, deeply integrating with the native managed services of Cloud providers is where much of the value of Cloud can be found; for other organizations, these patterns represent material lock-in risks that need to be mitigated.

Patterns and antipatterns

In software engineering, a software design pattern is a known solution to a class of problems in programming. An antipattern is a pattern that may be commonly used, but it is ineffective and counterproductive in practice.

The primary elements of developing for a Serverless-based application include these:

- Function logic is stateless.

- Functions are idempotent.

- There is just one task per function.

- Functions should finish as quickly as possible.

- Recursion should be avoided.

- You need to be aware of the concurrency problems with isolation and rate limits.

- Functions should avoid opening or minimize external network connections.

- The state is offloaded to an assumed Cloud storage.

Additionally, your serverless applications should follow one of the general patterns we discussed in Chapter 3:

- Consuming simple APIs via HTTP requests

- Fanning out the tasks into subtasks and fanning in the results from individual workers

- Using API Gateway as a proxy to encapsulated atomic Serverless functions

- Performing the gateway aggregation

- Publish-subscribe services using messages

- Queue-based load leveling

- The strangler pattern – a way of migrating a legacy system step by step by replacing existing functionalities with new services and serverless functions

- Read-intensive calls

- For processing streams and pipelines from IoT sensors or web UI clickstreams

At the very least, you should analyze candidate functions to avoid antipatterns and follow best practices:

- Assure clients are insensitive to function "cold-start" wait times.

- Do not include custom logging or trace resources for problem determination – good serverless platforms provide logging for you automatically as well as audit services.

- Do not do everything "from scratch" but leverage existing patterns and Cloud platform services.

- Use consistent, non-colliding naming conventions for functions.

- Utilize code source control systems and include code reviews and static analysis of the code. Also, add unit, function, and integration tests and execute them automatically at build time.

- Do not go the way of recursion.

- Look to use functions to tackle smaller, isolated parts when breaking down existing legacy applications while avoiding replacing stable centralized code.

Serverless benefits are still often misunderstood

What is often emphasized as the major advantage of serverless is that it is considerably cheaper to use than using infrastructure-based solutions. Many see serverless as a lightweight solution that can solve problems of a lightweight nature. But as we have demonstrated with use cases in this book, although the serverless architecture can be considered lightweight, it can easily handle any-size problems with major agglomeration of data every bit as large scale as the largest of the infrastructure-based use cases.[1] In addition, Serverless application development platforms provide almost total visibility into system and execution times and can aggregate the information systematically.

The Serverless patterns listed earlier are key to learning serverless computing from the ground up. Rather than starting with concepts, you start with running code which, since it is often open source, you are free to tweak and modify as you see fit. This will speed up the development process and ramp up your application delivery significantly.

---

[1]Resources for help:
```
https://aws.amazon.com/lambda/resources
https://developer.ibm.com/technologies/serverless/patterns/
```

Sometimes you might need to run your own deployment of Serverless – Apache OpenWhisk – in the enterprise in order to take advantage of your own infrastructure that is managed by your own organization. This is often the case in many industries due to regulatory and security concerns or where Public Cloud SLAs fall short.

As examples, medical providers have to consider requirements like the privacy of the patient or governmental agencies the handling of sensitive documents (civic or military alike). In many cases, it is often impossible to use Public Cloud data centers.

Running your own serverless platform may not be so bad, since you have access to trusted and proven codebases like Apache OpenWhisk which gives you access to a community of development resources and skills available as good as any in the market. Plus, well-managed open source projects always leverage the latest and greatest technologies available and have strict governance to assure quick turnarounds on bug fixes and security updates. Since Apache OpenWhisk is an Apache Software Foundation's Top-Level Project, you can be assured that it strives to be the best.

How to connect with authors and the technology

First of all, take part in the meetups that are being organized around the world. There are plenty of virtual meetups in the acceptable hours. Check all the world's locations and the biggest groups for the interesting themes of serverless. One of those meetups (`www.meetup.com/Serverless/`) is a good way to establish contacts within the global Serverless community.

Also you might want to follow developments of the framework here: `https://github.com/serverless-operations` – this Serverless Framework gives you everything you need to develop, deploy, monitor, and secure serverless applications on any Cloud.

Finally, you can become a committer of Apache project – and contribute to Apache OpenWhisk – check details here: `www.apache.org/dev/committers.html`.

There are some project meetings recorded on the Apache OpenWhisk YouTube channel: `www.youtube.com/channel/UCbzgShnQk8F43NKsvEYA1SA`.

You might also want to get the badge on Serverless using Developing Serverless Applications: A Practical Introduction with Apache OpenWhisk from `https://cognitiveclass.ai/courses`: Serverless Computing using Cloud Functions – Developer 1 course.

Also there is a free book available for download on Apache OpenWhisk with Node.js by our colleague Raymond Camden: *Developing Serverless Applications: A Practical Introduction with Apache OpenWhisk* – find out about it here: `www.raymondcamden.com/tags/openwhisk/`.

There is another book covering couple of the angles of using Apache OpenWhisk: *Learning Apache OpenWhisk: Developing Open Serverless Solutions 1st Edition* by Michele Sciabarrà (`www.amazon.com/Learning-Apache-OpenWhisk-Developing-Serverless/dp/1492046167`) (nothing on Swift though).

Finally, check the GitHub repository of this book here for the updated open source code and additional examples and resources.

About the authors and how to contact them

Lennart and Marek gathered together about 60 years of IT professional industry experience. For both of them, IT and technology is a life passion. It even led Marek to found his own startup in robotics and brought Lennart to undertake early AI research in Silicon Valley. And Northern California is where most of the time you might be able to meet Lennart and Marek in person, as they often present at various conferences in the United States and join various user groups globally on a variety of topics. See Figure 9-1 for a picture from their event in San Francisco. Lennart and Marek can be also reached at @LFrantzell @bluMarekS on Twitter or via email: serverless.swift@roboticsinventions.com.

Thank you for reading our book.

Figure 9-1. *At a meetup in San Francisco, from right Lennart and Marek*

APPENDIX A

Signing Up for the IBM Cloud Account

Sign up process

You will be using IBM Cloud with **a free of charge Lite account** in all the exercises provided in this book. In order to access IBM Cloud first, you need to sign up for a free Lite account. Then after confirming your email, you are ready to use the account.

Start simply by visiting page `https://bit.ly/serverless-swift-cloud-account`, which would redirect you to IBM Cloud signup page.

Fill out the provided signup form – see Figure A-1.

© Marek Sadowski and Lennart Frantzell 2020
M. Sadowski and L. Frantzell, *Serverless Swift*,
https://doi.org/10.1007/978-1-4842-5836-1

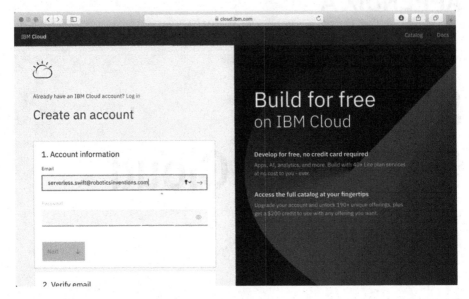

Figure A-1. *A signup screen for a free Lite account in IBM Cloud*

Confirm your email address that you provided via a verification code as shown in the email in Figure A-2.

Your IBM Cloud verification code

IBM **Cloud**

Hello,

Thank you for signing up for IBM Cloud!

Your 7-digit verification code is:

6653367

Enter this verification code on the IBM Cloud
registration page where you requested the
code. This code is valid for 30 minutes.

Welcome and happy building!

Thank you,
IBM Cloud

Visit the IBM Cloud console.
© Copyright IBM Corporation 2014, 2020.   IBM

Figure A-2. *IBM Cloud signup email with the verification code for a free Lite account*

After supplying the verification code, you should be able to finalize the
signup process and create the account like shown in Figure A-3.

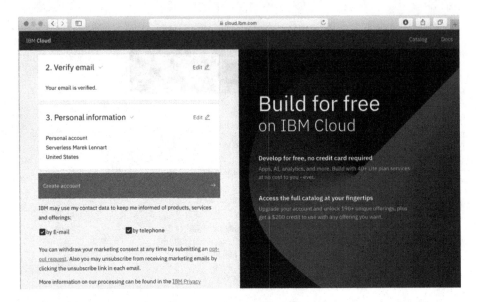

Figure A-3. *An IBM Cloud create account screen*

From now on when you visit the IBM Cloud using this link
`https://bit.ly/serverless-swift-dashboard`, you should be able to
see the Dashboard after you sign in as shown in Figure A-4.

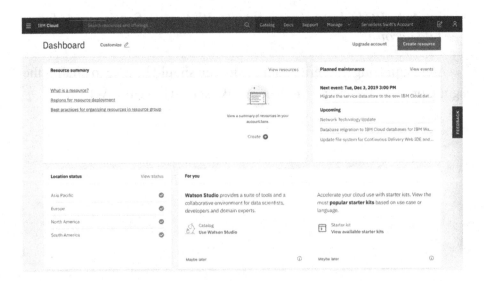

Figure A-4. *An IBM Cloud Dashboard*

When you access it for the first time, you might need to acknowledge processing of private information though. You would see something similar to the following screenshot in Figure A-5.

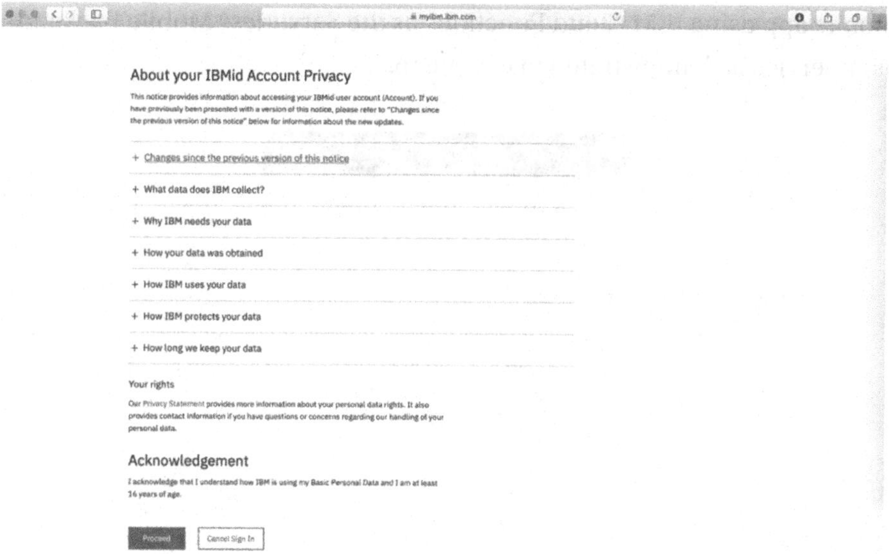

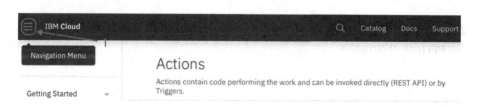

Figure A-5. *Acknowledging the private information processing*

Note   Always you are able to return to the Dashboard view by selecting a menu icon at the top left (also known as a hamburger) and selecting Dashboard (see Figure A-6).

Figure A-6. *Opening the menu with a click on the menu button (also known as a "hamburger")*

From this menu, you are able to select the IBM Cloud Functions console (see Figure A-7). The basic "Hello World" examples on using the IBM Cloud Functions are specified in Chapter 4. The details on using the IBM Cloud Functions are specified in Chapter 5. The full example of the mobile app using IBM Cloud Functions as the Serverless Mobile Backend-as-a-Service is demonstrated in Chapter 6.

Figure A-7. *Selecting the IBM Cloud Functions to work with your Serverless examples*

Congratulations! You claimed your free IBM Cloud account – the Lite account! From now on, you can write Serverless actions or test and develop various applications that are eligible for a Lite account. You might also want to upgrade to a pay-as-you-go account by adding the credit card information. In such a case, about 200 various paid services are available to you. Be prudent, the free monthly tier available in some of these services might be exhausted quickly, and you would end up paying for the used services.

Index

© Marek Sadowski and Lennart Frantzell 2020
M. Sadowski and L. Frantzell, *Serverless Swift*,
https://doi.org/10.1007/978-1-4842-5836-1

Printed in the United States
By Bookmasters